W9-AQI-110

Motorcycle Journeys Through the
American South

Scott Cochran

Whitehorse Press
Center Conway, New Hampshire

This book is dedicated to the two most important women in my life: my mother, Hassie Cochran, who taught me to love to read, and my wife Sylvia, who taught me the true meaning of love.

Whitehorse Press books are also available at discounts in bulk quantity for sales and promotional use. For details about special sales or for a catalog of motorcycling books, videos, and gear write to the publisher:
Whitehorse Press
107 East Conway Road
Center Conway, New Hampshire 03813
Phone: 603-356-6556 or 800-531-1133
E-mail: CustomerService@WhitehorsePress.com
Internet: www.WhitehorsePress.com

ISBN 978-1-884313-61-5

5 4 3 2 1

Printed in China

Acknowledgments

Special thanks go out to the staff at USRiderNews who took up my slack while I was out researching rides; Gerbings, who provided me with heated clothing so I could finish this book on time; and to everyone who contributed in some small measure to make this book possible: Anna, Trae, Jeff, Joey, Carol, Paul, Meruice, Peggy, and my son Jason.

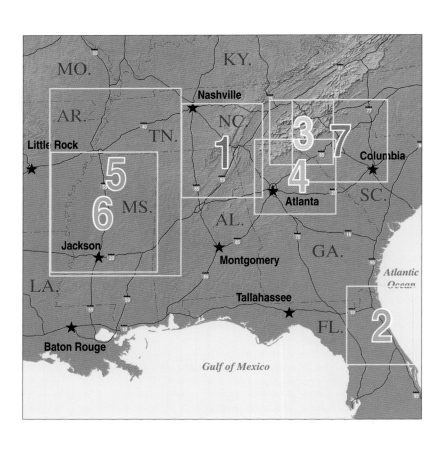

Contents

Introduction

Welcome to my first book, *Motorcycle Journeys through the American South*. I appreciate the opportunity to introduce you to the joys of two wheel travel through the land of my birth. Having grown up in tiny Keysville, Georgia, in the Central Savannah River area, I am at home on the back roads and byways of this region. Discovering secluded swimming holes, meeting interesting people, and locating restaurants with local flavor is second nature to me, and something I enjoy.

The Talladega Parkway doesn't attract the crowds that the more well known parkways of the mid-Atlantic region do. So there will be times during the changing of the seasons where you'll have the panoply of colors all to yourself. Enjoy!

The entrance to Little River Canyon Parkway on Hwy 176 which is known as Lookout Mountain Parkway. For years this stretch of highway was the worst paved, best road to ride in Alabama, but thanks to the recent resurfacing job, this road has been elevated to my top ten in the American South.

While I won't show you the swimming holes I found, I will take you on a journey through a region that still adheres to and honors the values and traditions handed down from generation to generation. In this book I hope to introduce you to some of the people who have shaped the very fabric of our southern society, and take you on some of the best motorcycle roads south of the Mason Dixon line.

In any motorcycle travel guide there are three types of journeys. One will have a challenging road that will excite and delight you with all its twists and turns, but otherwise has little to recommend it. The second type is full of adventure and discovery with an engaging history or a must-see attraction, but pretty bland as motorcycle roads go. The third, and rarest of all, combines the previous two. You will find all three types of rides in this book, and I think you'll enjoy them all.

I took this photo of myself riding by using a remote camera switch. Right after this shot, someone riding by saw my camera on the tripod and stopped to retrieve it, thinking someone had left a perfectly good camera on the side of the road. Luckily I returned in time to assure the finder that the camera wasn't really lost!

It includes journeys in Florida that will help you escape the Daytona Bike Week madness, find mountains, and sit down for a meal in the state's oldest diner, if not the South's. We'll visit a town used by pirates hiding out from the King's navy, and it's not St. Augustine. Together we'll ride for two days on the old Natchez Trace Parkway and search for the lost Roxie Hole gold. We'll travel to the Blues Crossroads and if we're lucky sit in on a jam session with local bluesmen. We'll sample a fried green tomato *sammich* in an authentic southern juke joint and try out the barbeque in Central Mississippi. Along the way we'll spend the night in a sharecropper's cabin on what was once a working southern plantation.

We'll visit a petrified forest and listen to the secrets of an alligator as we hunt the Ma Barker Gang. We'll stand at the rim of Georgia's Little Grand Canyon and witness the awesome power of nature, find the highest point in Georgia, and then eat lunch at a southern restaurant where Thomas Edison, Henry Ford, Lady Bird Johnson, and Walt Disney once dined. You and I will visit the home of our 39th President, Jimmy Carter, and have our picture taken standing behind a wooden peanut. For Elvis fans, we'll journey to the place of his birth and step inside his tiny boyhood home, eat lunch in the actual unrestored Drive-In he frequented after school, and stand in the same spot in the still thriving hardware store where his mamma bought him his first guitar.

In this small tome, there is no way I could completely cover the vastness that is the American South. With an area that encompasses 11 states, the American South is rich in its history and diverse in its culture. I have endeavored to provide you with a broad sampling of what the American South is today and what has defined our past. I hope you will come away with an appreciation of what the region has to offer you as a motorcycle traveler.

The astute reader may notice that the State of Louisiana isn't represented. We have Hurricane Katrina to thank for that. The devastation inflicted on the Gulf Coast and the New Orleans area forced me at the last minute to change my plans since I had no way to know if many of the places and towns that I had visited would still be open in the aftermath. If there is a second edition to this book I promise to include that area.

I hope you enjoy reading this book as much as I have enjoyed writing it for you. As a bonus, you can visit *USRiderNews* (www.usridernews.com/book.html) and download detailed maps, view more photos, and contribute comments about your experiences as you visit the places listed in the book. If I've left out your favorite road or destination, tell me where it is and what's special about it; who knows, it might show up in a later edition.

Remember to ride safe, and always take the road less traveled.

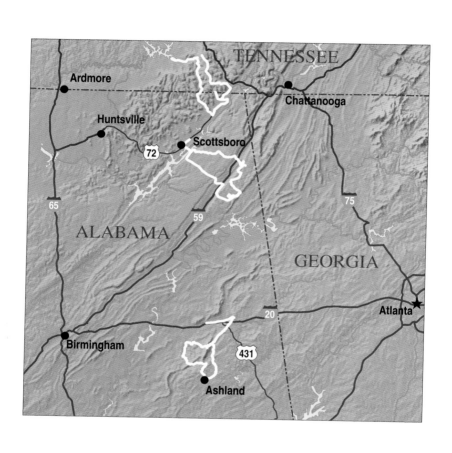

Sweet Home

Don't Let Anyone Tell You Alabama Is All Flat!

To my way of reckoning, there are four distinct regions of Alabama. There is the coastal Alabama that includes Mobile, Dauphin Island, and Gulf Shores. In the initial outline of this book I intended to include rides from this area but Hurricane Katrina spoiled those plans. I've enjoyed riding the coastal areas of Alabama, Mississippi, and Louisiana but after the devastation, I decided to save it for another time. In addition to the Coastal region there is the River Heritage region, the Metropolitan region, and the Mountain region. We'll take several rides from the Mountain region and one from the Metropolitan region.

On the Talladega Parkway the fall colors arrive late in the year due to the moderate temperatures and are often more subtle and muted than those encountered along the Blue Ridge or Skyline Drive. But, there's something to be said for our southern climate which provides enough warm days to ride year round!

For football fans, Alabama is best known as the home of legendary Bear Bryant. When I was growing up, Coach Paul William "Bear" Bryant was a familiar sight on the sidelines in his hound's-tooth hat. While football doesn't have much to do with touring by motorcycle, I would be remiss if I didn't pay homage to the man from Alabama who was simply the best there ever was, at least in the football arena. To my readers from outside the South, you should understand this. If you're passing through some small town on Friday night and it seems deserted, chances are better than even that everyone's at the football stadium near the high school. Also, if you're planning a trip through the South during football season you'd be well advised to check the college calendar so you don't find yourself in a college town on game day without a hotel reservation and no hope of securing one.

One word of advice to those of you who will follow me on the routes outlined in this book. If you find yourself in a football discussion with a local and he or she endeavors to elicit your opinion as to your favorite football team, I heartily encourage you to remain neutral. It's best to simply sigh and say, "Oh, I don't really follow football that much." Although your response will result in a look of disbelief from the other person, it will save you from picking the wrong team and then wondering if the locals are fixing to ride you out on a rail, right after they tar and feather you. Even I, a native son of the South, sometimes use this when in unfamiliar territory!

Besides football, Alabama lays claim to a wealth of natural beauty and the mountains in the northern part of the state hold some of the best motorcycle riding areas in the region. Just south of the Tennessee line we'll ride Lookout Mountain, one of my favorite areas, and then visit the southernmost ski resort in the country where the ground shook in a California style honest-to-goodness earthquake.

And speaking of earth shattering, motorcycle enthusiasts who are also amateur anthropologists will have to visit Desoto Falls to see for themselves if Columbus was actually centuries late in discovering America! The locals in northeastern Alabama claim there is evidence that a Welsh Prince established a settlement in this area a couple hundred years *before* Columbus ever set sail. If that's true then I know a few history books that will need to be updated. I can't attest to the veracity of the claim, but then again, poking around in damp caves and digging up bones isn't how I like to spend my free time.

From there we'll head toward the center of the state to Mt. Cheaha, a short drive from the capitol of Birmingham and a few hours west of the *hub of the south,* Atlanta, Georgia.

Mt. Cheaha offers the motorcycle traveler scenic overlooks and in the fall changing colors that rival the better known vistas of the Blue Ridge Parkway.

Upon This Rock. This 1930s-era chapel was built around a boulder which serves as the pulpit. Although small by modern standards, it's a favorite location for romantic weddings because of the story of its builder, his love for his first wife and the second wife who helped him secure the funds to complete this building dedicated to his first wife, and later had his ashes interred into the boulder inside. Yes, it's a little confusing, I admit.

Then there's the Natchez Trace Parkway which cuts across the northwestern tip of Alabama. The Natchez Trace is explored in another chapter in this book, but it bears mentioning here because it provides the motorcycle tourer with yet another excuse to set aside the time to come and explore the region.

Besides the natural wonders awaiting you in Alabama, there will be abundant opportunities for you to sample authentic southern cuisine. And speaking of southern food, be sure to visit the Western Sizzlin' Steakhouse on John T. Reid Parkway in Scottsboro, Alabama, for breakfast. If they're still doing a breakfast buffet, they'll most likely have fried bologna. If you've never had it, you're in for an authentic southern treat that is fast disappearing from our kitchens in favor of more healthful fare. While we're on that subject, the next time you're out for a ride and happen upon an old church with a cemetery that dates back to the 1800s, take a few minutes and look at all the headstones with our ancestors who lived well into their 80s and 90s. Now I know that life expectancy overall has increased but isn't it odd that these folks ate pork in almost everything, drank whole milk, and consumed a lot of unhealthy foods, yet those who died a natural death (not accidental or war-related) seemed to live so much longer than we do today? My point is, don't blame the bologna!

As with any travel adventure, lodging is important. For the most part I tend to stick to the boring but predictable chain hotels when I travel. While that's not very romantic, I need wireless internet at the end of the day to help me co-ordinate my day job as editor of *USRiderNews*. Often the bed and breakfast establishments mentioned in this book do not cater to the business traveler and therefore haven't found it necessary to provide internet service. That's also why I don't camp when I'm traveling. With that being said, if you're traveling for the express purpose of getting away from all the static of modern life, then by all means skip the chains and seek the off-the-beaten-path hotels and bed-and-breakfast establishments. In Valley Head there is an authentic southern ante-bellum bed-and-breakfast, The Winston House. In nearby Mentone, you'll find the Mentone Springs Hotel. Both are clean and wonderfully charming places to stay. On the "Bologna and Ice Cream" route you'll pass through Cow-an, Tennessee, where the Franklin-Pearson House stands. It's at 108 Cumber-land Street and rooms start at $90 per night. At the highest point in Alabama, on the Mt. Cheaha loop, the option is to stay at the State Park either in one of the cabins or the hotel. The hotel rooms start at $68 for peak season (except

You won't find this franchise in Pittsburg, Pennsylvania, but you should stop and sample the ice cream or a Dagwood Sandwich at this Dixie Freeze in South Pittsburg, Tennessee.

Taking the time to enjoy the natural beauty of the American South is an important aspect of two wheel travel. You should allow yourself time to spend in quiet solitude whenever the opportunity presents itself.

race weekends) and $55 off peak season. The cabins and chalets range from $100 to $1,150 per night depending on the size and the season.

Whatever your choices, Alabama beckons you to explore its rich heritage and great riding roads.

Trip 1 Fried Bologna and Ice Cream

Distance *140 miles*
Terrain *Two lane roads through rural farmland. Tight twisting mountain switchbacks. Wide sweeping curves and views of the Cumberland Plateau. Traffic is light to moderate.*
Highlights *Fried bologna, High Rock Overlook, Natural Bridge, Walls of Jericho, railroad museum, castle, primitive cave, ice cream, and twisty mountain roads*

Using **Scottsboro** as a hub, we'll ride the foothills of the southern Appalachian Mountains and explore the area that was vital to the South during the War Between the States.

This adventure can begin even before you leave town as my favorite breakfast spot is an unusual one. The **Western Sizzlin' Steakhouse** (256-259-6888) isn't known for its breakfast food, but this particular one at 23980 John T Reid Pkwy (US 72) offers up a $3.99 breakfast buffet bar (drink included) that is the best value within 100 miles. Besides the price, the cooks here sling a southern delicacy that you simply have to stop and sample. No, it's not grits! That's a

It's always a good idea to ask the locals where they like to ride. That's how I first discovered serpentine State Route 35 which winds up Scraper Mountain.

tired stereotypical travel menu item that only serves to show the locals how little you know about real southern culture. Instead, if you want to fit in and sound like a true blue Southerner, you have to eat the fried bologna. In case you don't know (and most of you don't), bologna is a sandwich meat, either pork or beef, processed from—uh, how can I say this nicely—just about anything and everything edible from the animal. It's technically a sausage and as Otto von Bismarck said "If you like laws and sausage, you should never watch either being made." While I will admit that the cholesterol count in fried bologna is somewhere just shy of an instant heart attack, the flavor is pure southern, and something you have to try whenever you see it on the menu, or in this case, on the breakfast buffet. Go ahead, one piece won't kill you.

The best time to see the entire Cumberland Plateau is in the winter after the foliage has disappeared. On this route you'll have a couple of opportunities to experience this vista!

With your fill of bologna, start out at the intersection of Hwy 72/2 and SR 35 (Veterans Drive). Reset your odometer here and drive north on SR 35 for one mile into the downtown area. We'll explore later, so continue straight at the stoplight across the tracks onto CR 21. The road starts bending suggestively for a few miles but keep your throttle hand loose, the real twisties will arrive shortly. At 6.1 miles continue straight onto CR 470. As you leave the city, the land on either side of the narrow two-lane road turns into rural farm land. In early spring, the farmers plant corn and cotton and by the fall, many of these fields will be white and ready to harvest. At Mile 7.7 turn left onto CR 33, which the locals tout as one of the five best motorcycle roads in Alabama. I could agree with them except for one thing, the road surface. For twisting and torturous spiral blacktop, this section of Alabama is as good as any; however the road surface desperately needed improving when I was last there. A little fresh asphalt would elevate this ride to the top three in Alabama. You'll see what I mean three miles later as you start to climb Scraper Hill. No, I didn't make that name up, it's on the official map of the area, and it's appropriate. Switchbacks, off camber turns, tight decreasing radius turns will have you scraping your pegs and pipes for the next several miles.

You may wonder why I chose to ride this section uphill instead of reversing my route and enjoying this section downhill. That's because I made Scottsboro my base and I knew that if I really wanted, I could turn around and ride it again. You see, I believe that the only thing better than riding a twisty mountain road once, is riding it again in the opposite direction. Anyway, you'll have the opportunity to return this way at the end of this journey if you choose.

THE ROUTE FROM SCOTTSBORO

0   Start on SR 35 at US 72

1.0   Continue straight across railroad tracks to CR 21 (Tupelo Pike Road)

6.1   Continue straight onto CR 470

7.7   Turn left on CR 33

19.2   Turn right on SR 79

28.7   Cross state line into Tennessee—road becomes SR 16 (Rowe Gap Road)

45.8   Turn right onto US 64 (Veterans Memorial Drive)

48.9   Take ramp right heading into Cowan

49.2   At top of ramp, turn right

58.4   Turn right onto SR 56 (Sherwood Road)

60.7   Turn left on Natural Bridge Road

61.4   Parking area for Natural Bridge—depart and return to SR 56

62.0   Turn left back onto SR 56 (Sherwood Road)

69.7   Youngs Creek Road, Gager Lime Manufacturing, castle ruins

76.0   Cross state line into Alabama—road becomes SR 117

89.5   Turn left on US 72/SR 2

98.5   Turn left on CR 75 toward Russell Cave

101.0 Go straight on US 72/CR 75

101.4 Turn left on CR 98 to Russell Cave

105.0 Entrance to cave on left

109.0 Retrace route to US 72 and turn left

115.8 Turn left on 3rd Street in South Pittsburg

115.9 Turn right on Elm Street to Dixie Freeze

116.0 Turn left on SR 156

140.3 End at US 41A in St. Andrews

Hold onto your sheets. Local legend has it that the express trains were so fast that when they passed the railroad depot hotel (brick building), the windows would open and the rush of air would pull the sheets right off the bed. Don't believe me? Then read the sign for yourself!

At Mile 19.2, turn right onto SR 79. In just over nine miles you'll cross into Tennessee and the road name will change to TN16. Just before crossing the state line you'll see a sign for the Walls of Jericho on your left and a driveway through a yellow gate into a gravel parking lot. Davey Crockett's family once lived in the vicinity of this landmark (Tennesseans call him **David Crockett**). The area referred to as the **"Walls of Jericho"** is a bowl-shaped natural amphitheater that shoots water out of holes and cracks in the canyon wall during times of high flow. For the truly adventurous, this excursion will test your physical endurance, but if you're up to it, the trip to the gorge is worth the three and a half mile hike (one way). This isn't for the faint of heart and since a seven mile hike might take all day, I suggest you pack a lunch.

As you continue north along this section of Hwy 16 (also known as Rowe Gap Road), the highway begins climbing toward the top of the Cumberland Plateau and becomes a joy to ride. Long, slow sweepers come quick enough to keep any rider from becoming bored but tame enough to be enjoyed by die-hard cruiser riders intent on absorbing as much of their surroundings as possible.

Soon you'll finish the climb and start descending toward the town of **Cowan** and the valley below. At certain times of the year when the vegetation is dormant, the view opens up and you can glimpse the Cumberland Valley spread out in all its majesty. It's a view that will be repeated again on the other side of Cowan.

At Mile 45.8, turn right (East) onto US 64 (Veterans Memorial Drive). Three miles later you'll take the off ramp to the right for US 41A (Cowan Highway). At the top of the ramp turn right to travel southeast into the town of Cowan proper.

If you're hungry for lunch, stop in at **Buck's Market** (415 West Cumberland, 931-967-6241) for a plate of barbeque or perhaps to sample a fried pie, a local favorite. If authentic southern barbeque ain't to your liking, there is the **Corner House** (401 East Cumberland Street, 931-967-3910) for dining in a Victorian setting, or my favorite, **Trisha's Memories** (107 East Cumberland, 931-967-4467) an old-time ice cream shop located downtown in an old cafe. Trisha serves up home-style shakes, malts, cones, and (believe it or not) authentic Cajun cooking.

Railroad buffs will have to stop in at the Cowan Railroad Museum in Cowan, Tennessee, open May through October, Thursday through Sunday.

For railroad buffs, the **Cowan Railroad Museum** (www.visitcowan.com) is open from May until October, Thursday through Saturday (excluding holidays) 10 to 4 p.m., and on Sundays from 1 to 4 p.m. Admission is free and inside you'll find a large collection of railroad relics, and memorabilia. Outside there is an authentic steam locomotive, flatcar, and caboose. Also, a replica of the county's first courthouse stands a few feet from the museum on the downtown square. During the holiday season, the locals often decorate the square

This natural stone bridge near the town of Cowan, Tennessee, offers a chance to get off the bike and enjoy a few minutes with nature. If you sit still long enough, and keep your eyes sharp enough, you might just see a fox or bobcat.

with lights and plastic snowmen like many small towns, but the most curious thing to me was the fake snow and red ribbon on the structure and on the lighted Christmas tree inside. I'm fairly certain this isn't an authentic recreation of how this courthouse looked in the 1800s. It appeared so odd to me that I took a photograph just to show my riding buddies. The funny part is several of them told me they thought it looked fine. Hmmm.

If you're looking for a romantic getaway in Cowan, **The Franklin-Pearson House** (108 East Cumberland Street, www.franklinpearson.com, 931-962-3223), built in 1850 as a railroad hotel, was restored in 2003 as an authentic turn of the century bed-and-breakfast inn. It is two stories and has nine rooms ($90 to 140 per night).

As you leave Cowan continue traveling southeasterly on 41A up the mountain. At Mile 56, you'll pass through a pair of stone gates and immediately on your left will be a pulloff at a large stone outcropping. Access to the top of this 30 foot monolith is via a set of stairs cut into the stone. I don't know who cut the stairs or what agency oversees its use, but there are no handrails or idiot barriers separating you from a 50-foot drop to the forest floor below. How refreshing! Carved into and painted all over the stone are the names and initials of lovers both recent and from years past. A fair portion of these would probably be from the nearby educational institution of **Sewanee, The University of the South.** Those daring to climb to the top are rewarded with a panoramic view of the Cumberland Plateau that on a clear day easily exceeds 50 miles or more. The "fall color" tourists clog this road in the leaf changing season, but most times the highway traffic is light to moderate. As you leave, continue on US 41A up the mountain.

At Mile 58.4, turn right onto SR 56 (Sherwood Road). Don't get in a hurry though because at Mile 60.7, turn left on the Natural Bridge Road and drive one mile to a parking area. Park your bike, and walk down the well maintained steps. In 50 feet you'll find the **Natural Bridge,** a stone formation which gets its name from its bridge-like shape. Spanning approximately 30 to 40 feet over the forest floor, the "bridge" juts out from the side of the mountain into the lush forest canopy. There isn't a stream below, so you can easily hike down to the area underneath. On a recent trip, I discovered the fresh, half-eaten remains of a squirrel, which indicated some type of predator in the area. It could've been a fox, or a dog, but it also could have been a wild mountain lion so I don't recommend taking a nap under the stone outcroppings located at the base of the "bridge!"

After you've relaxed and taken in your fill of the scenery, retrace your route to Hwy 56 and turn left at Mile 62. For the next few miles, the snake-like turns on this section of highway will temp you to twist the throttle. In a few miles, you'll come into the town of **Sherwood**. While you won't see any knights or

Is that a damsel in distress upon yonder parapet? If it is, then she's trespassing in the dilapidated ruins of the Gager Lime Manufacturing Company. Built in the 1800s these now crumbling storage silos were designed to resemble castle walls. Maybe their creators were inspired by the fact that the plant sits on "Sherwood Road?"

knaves nearby (forgive me, I just couldn't help it) you will see the ruins of a castle. At Mile 69.7 (Youngs Creek Road) stands what remains of **Gager Lime Manufacturing Company,** constructed in the late 1800s. Plant engineer George Kinney designed the storage silos of the plant to resemble castle parapet walls. Other buildings feature stylized "papyriform" pilasters surrounding the window bays to resemble ancient Egypt. The business closed in 1949 and the concrete buildings are now crumbling, slowly returning the lime back into the surrounding soil from whence it was once mined.

At Mile 76, you'll cross back into Alabama and the road changes to SR 117. Shortly you'll enter the town of **Stevenson.** History buffs will want to stop in at the renovated railroad depot and hotel, next to the train tracks (where else?).

It's said the hotel was so close to the tracks that passing trains would cause the hotel windows to open and pull the sheets right off the beds! The tracks are still in use, but the hotel is used for various other businesses.

You'll need to turn right to remain on SR 117. At Mile 89.5, you'll reach US 72/SR 2 (Lee Highway). Turn left, and one mile later, bear left on SR 2 Old Hwy 72. At Mile 98.5, turn left on CR 98 to reach **Russell Cave National Monument** which contains the largest and most complete archeological records of human habitation in this part of the country, dating back more than 9,000 years. This is an undeveloped cave, which means you have to supply your own light, hardhat or helmet, and first aid kit (which you should have on your bike with you at all times). Stop at the visitors center for a permit. Only three people at a time are allowed inside. If you're used to the touristy-type caves, this one will open your eyes to what real cavers do. Depending on how much of the cave you explore, you may have to wade through water and navigate some tight passageways. It's not for everyone, but it is very interesting.

When you're finished, turn right on CR 98 and approximately four miles later, turn left on US 72.

At Mile 115.8, turn left on 3rd Street for one block and then right on Elm Avenue. On your left is the **Dixie Freeze.** In business since the 50s, this icon is well known throughout the area. As the sign says, the house specialty is the "dagwood" sandwich. You have to try one. The ice cream isn't half-bad either.

Leave the Dixie Freeze and turn left on SR 156 at Mile 116. The last leg of this adventure is a challenging two-lane twisty road through the **Franklin-Marion State Park.** At the time this area was acquired from a coal mining company in the 1930s, it was an ecological disaster. Today, the scars are still there but time and Mother Nature have healed many of its wounds. You'll be glad because I really did save the best road for last. Our journey ends at Mile 140 at US 41A. If you have time, turn left and visit Sewanee, The University of The South. Cruise around this picturesque campus and take time to visit one last overlook to end the day's adventure.

If you've made Scottsboro your base, retrace your steps through Cowan, turn left on SR 16 (Rowe Gap Road) remembering that it changes back into SR 79 when you cross back into Alabama. You can turn left on CR 33 and enjoy that section of wonderful spiral wiggles a second time before arriving back in Scottsboro.

Trip 2   The Earthquake Capitol of the South

Distance   *104 miles*

Terrain   *Flat at first. A nice, twisty, two-lane road as you descend Little Mountain to Desoto Falls. Then finally, you're rewarded with eleven miles of curves along the Little River Canyon Parkway and some dangerous 700-foot dropoffs without guard rails. Traffic is moderate to heavy depending on the season.*

Highlights   *An authentic southern mansion, a cave named for an Indian Maid, Desoto Falls, site of the first European settlers, twisty blacktop in Little River Canyon State Park, and the home of one of country music's living legends.*

Hernando de Soto visited this area and this waterfall bears his name. But, that's not the whole story. There is evidence that a Welsh Prince actually arrived here several hundred years before de Soto or Columbus! The controversy is explained in detail at the site of Desoto Falls.

Since Scottsboro is our base for this ride, we'll start in the same spot, where SR 35 intersects with US 72.

The small town of **Scottsboro,** Alabama, has a population of 15,000 and is located in the northeast corner of Alabama, along the **Tennessee River.** For the history buff, Scottsboro is well-known as the location of the infamous legal saga of the **Scottsboro Boys.** In March of 1931, nine black males were convicted and sentenced to death for raping two white girls on a slow moving freight train between Chattanooga, Tennessee, and Paint Rock, Alabama. The case, widely publicized throughout the nation during the Great Depression, was unusual in that the NAACP (National Association for the Advancement of Colored People) did not rush to defend the accused. Rather, it was the Communist Party's legal defense arm, the ILD (International Labor Defense) that represented the boys. You can imagine how that went over in rural America! Several books, and at least one made-for-TV-movie, *Judge Horton and the Scottsboro Boys,* recounted the tragic events of this period in southern history.

Take SR 35 at its intersection with US 72 and head east. In 3.3 miles, turn left on SR 40/117. Continue for 24 miles and at Mile 27.3, turn right, travel a few hundred yards on US 11/SR 117, and then turn left on SR 117 toward the town of Valley Head. If you're hungry or just like homemade desserts, on your right stands **Shorty's Cafe** (37757 Highway 11, Hammondville, 256-635-0245). Open from 10 to 8 p.m. Monday through Saturday, Shorty's is just the kind of down home no-frills cafe that beckons you with genuine southern hospitality and authentic home cooked food. I recently stopped in while checking mileage for this book and a friendly back-and-forth fired up between one of the locals and a couple of the waitresses. Since it was obvious I was a visitor, the local leaned over to me and quipped, "These waitresses will treat you so many different ways you're bound to like one of them!" After listening to them toss barbs back and forth, I have to say I'm glad I wasn't a local! If you stop in, ask how Shorty came to be called Shorty, since she's of average height.

Driving on SR 117 you'll enter the town of **Valley Head** almost without warning. Besides its natural beauty, Valley Head is quite often the coldest spot in Alabama during the winter months. In February of 1905 the mercury plunged to 18 degrees below zero! Hopefully it's warmer when you ride through. If you have the time you might stop to tour **Winston Place B & B**

THE ROUTE FROM SCOTTSBORO

0	Start on SR 35 and US 72/SR 2
3.3	Turn left on SR 40
27.3	Turn right on SR 117
27.4	Turn left on SR 117 toward Valley Head
31.7	Turn right on CR 89 in Mentone
33.9	Turn left on CR 613 to Desoto Falls
35.6	Return to CR 89 and turn left
39.1	Turn left on CR 89 to CR 165 (Webster Road)
40.1	Arrive at Howard Chapel on right
41.0	Return on CR 165 to CR 89 and turn left on Lookout Mountain Parkway
46.7	Turn left on SR 35
52.0	Turn right on SR 176 (Little River Canyon Parkway)
67.0	Go straight on CR 81
70.6	Turn right on US 11 (North Valley Avenue)
77.0	Turn left (or right depending if you went downtown) on SR 35
104.0	Arrive at starting point in Scottsboro SR 35 and US 72

Winston Bed and Breakfast survived the Civil War because its owner, Colonel William Winston, as a member of the Secession Convention, voted against Secession. The Union General who briefly occupied it decided to spare the structure as a reward for his loyalty to the union.

($125 to $150, 888-494-6786) located one block east of your route on Railroad Avenue. Built in 1831, this is an authentic *Gone With the Wind*-era **southern mansion.** While it's no Tara, the structure does exude the aura of genteel southern charm. The house was briefly occupied by the Union Army during the War Between the States and the only reason it was spared the torch was because its owner, **Colonel William O. Winston,** a member of the **Secession Convention,** voted not to secede at the start of the war movement. Because of this, the Union Brigadeer General **Jefferson C. Davis** (no relation to the President of the Confederacy) ordered that the house and outbuildings be spared. But lest there be any doubt as to the sacrifice the Winston's made to the Confederacy, both Winston sons, Will and George, died in battle and are buried on the property. Tours are $5 and are conducted daily.

Leaving Valley Head, you'll climb **Lookout Mountain** to the town of **Mentone** (www.mentonealabama.org). As you climb to the town you'll probably notice a mile long stone wall on your left. In 1927–28, the citizens of Mentone built this "guardrail" to protect visiting tourists from sliding off the side of the mountain in their new fangled automobiles, probably when the temperature dipped below zero heading into Valley Head!

The oldest hotel in Alabama is in pretty good shape for her age. How old is she? The Mentone Springs Hotel was built in 1884 and used for generations as a summer retreat. The best time to visit Mentone is in the spring or fall.

At the end of the wall, the road bends right and you're in Mentone. If you have a few minutes to spare, you will probably want to stop and learn a little of the history of what was once a bustling vacation retreat. Two very large hotels remain as testament to a time when those with the economic means would travel by train to Valley Head and vacation during the "summer" in Mentone. For overnight accommodations, there is the **Mentone Springs Hotel** (www.mentonespringshotel.com), which lays claim as the oldest hotel in Alabama. If you're hungry, there are two restaurants in the hotel. **Caldwell's Restaurant,** open Friday and Saturday nights and Sunday for brunch, is slightly formal and reservations during the tourist season would be a wise decision. For a more relaxed atmosphere the **Rusty Fox Cafe** is the choice. The pork tenderloin hoagie is worth ordering. During the season, the **Log Cabin Deli and Craft Village** beckon you to pause, enjoy the ambiance, and perhaps spread around a few of your hard earned greenbacks. In the early 1800s, the **Deli** restaurant (Lookout Mountain, Mentone, 256-634-4560) was supposedly an Indian Trading Post. Try the Cabin Cooler, an unusual concoction that I can only describe as Siberian iced tea. Chances are most of my readers won't be interested in doing a little snow skiing, but just so you'll know, Mentone is also home to the southernmost ski resort in the USA, the **Cloudmont Ski and Golf Resort and Shady Grove Dude Ranch.** Call for more info 256-634-4344.

At Mile 31.7, you'll turn right onto the Desoto Parkway (CR 89) and wind down **Little Mountain.** A few miles later you'll pass Comer Scout Road, home to **Camp Comer.** In the spring and summer months, thousands of young boys and girls converge on the area to fill up this camp and the dozen other youth camps in the area. Camp Comer easily holds 500 campers at one time.

This stretch of road has residential dwellings that line both sides of the narrow two-lane piece of blacktop and can be quite busy during the peak seasons. Be ever vigilant for four-wheel cages turning left into driveways or backing out of driveways in front of you.

At Mile 33.9, turn left onto CR 613 to head to **Desoto Falls,** named for the famous Spanish explorer **Hernando de Soto.** While there is little doubt that he visited this area, it is the tantalizing evidence in nearby caves that may one day re-write the history books. It seems some historians and researchers believe that the **Welsh Prince Madoc (Mad Dog)** arrived here several hundred years *before* Columbus discovered the Americas. It's a source of pride among some locals that it's highly possible that the fortifications in the caves high above Desoto Falls were built by Welsh settlers. A Tennessee Governor in the late 1700s gave additional evidence from an old Cherokee chief of a tale among his people about a Welsh prince that fought with the Cherokee. The discovery in 1799 of skeletons wearing armor and a breastplate adorned with a Welsh seal served to affirm the believers and confound the skeptics. The State of Alabama maintains the site, but as a general rule, you can't visit the caves to see the evidence for yourself. However if you're a serious archeologist type, there's always a way to get permission. Check with the local authorities. Tell them I sent you. That'll get you nowhere, but it's better than nothing.

In 1.1 miles you'll arrive at the parking area. There is an overlook with a generous view of the actual falls. In the spring and summer the water volume is much higher than in the winter. The dam you see was constructed in the early 1900s to give the locals electricity. It is no longer in use for power generation.

Retrace your route to CR 89 and at Mile 35.6, turn left. At Mile 39.1, turn left on CR 165. In one mile you'll come to a most unusual church with a huge boulder as its pulpit. The **Sallie Howard Memorial Chapel** was built in 1937 by Milford W. Howard with help from the Civilian Conservation Corp. This working church stands as mute testament to one man's love for his first wife

Sequoyah Caverns

For an interesting side trip visit nearby **Sequoyah Caverns** (www. sequoyahcaverns.com, 800-843-5098). Admission is $10.95 per adult. Just after you pass the interstate, turn left at Mile 27.3 on US 11. At 32.9 turn left on CR 371 and in a mile you'll come to the cave entrance. The fact that the caverns are named after the famous American Indian Sequoyah is pure marketing because there's no evidence she had any connection with them. So, why the name? For about a century this geological feature was known as Ellis Cave. In April 1964 Clark Byers, who had a genius for marketing, leased the cave from the Jones family and changed the name to Sequoyah Cave. If the name change doesn't sound to you like the work of a marketing genius, then how's this: Byers also painted all those barns with the slogan "See Rock City." Yes, I thought you'd agree with me. The tour guide at the caverns will point out a signature that is purported to be General Sam Houston, but I can't verify that. For a short time during the cold war, the local Civil Defense stocked provisions in the caverns on the off chance the world would end abruptly in nuclear holocaust. After visiting, I'm not sure I'd want to live underground for the rest of my life, or at least until the supplies ran out, but I guess it beats the alternative. If you take this detour, you will need to add 15.2 miles to your total when you return to Shorty's Cafe at SR 117 and US 11.   ■

and a second wife's love for the same man. Howard was born in Rome and became a successful lawyer and speaker and eventually married Sallie Lankford. After retiring due to illness, he made a series of investments that went south. Financially broke, the two moved to California. He eventually returned to Mentone and began work on a school for underprivileged children, while Sallie remained in California and regularly sent money to Milford. She came east for a summer, but ill with cancer returned to California and soon died. Without her financial support, the school was not finished. Shortly thereafter Milford married Stella "Lady Vivian" Harper who helped him get the funds necessary to build this church which he dedicated to his first wife. The Chapel was dedicated June 1937 and Howard died in California in December of that same year. Lady Vivian brought Howard's ashes home and had them interred in the huge boulder inside the church in 1938. A bronze plaque on the boulder reads "Milford W. Howard, born December 18, 1867. Died December 28, 1937. I shall dwell in the house of the Lord forever."

Retrace your path a couple hundred yards north to CR 165 and **Desoto Parkway.** You'll enter and exit the park on this highway. At Mile 46.1, you'll turn left on SR 35, Wallace Avenue. If you're a catfish or shrimp lover, directly in front of you stands **JT's Fish House** (1907 Scenic Road, East Fort Payne, 256-997-0459). The building is painted lime green in reverence to their specialty, Key Lime Pie, and it won't disappoint you. The shrimp and catfish are farm raised in nearby **Utah,** Alabama, in a pond injected with 20 percent saline. This gives a unique flavor to both the shrimp and catfish and one I can promise you will enjoy. There are also frog legs and spicy fried pickle spears! The building and land is owned by **Jeff Owens** of the musical group, Alabama, and he comes in sometimes on the weekend. Depending on the day JT's has live music or karaoke, which is kind of live, depending on the singer. They are open Monday through Friday for lunch from 10:30 to 2 p.m., and for dinner

Wild and untamed, the Little River Gorge cuts through northern Alabama. With overlooks 700 feet high and few guardrails along this route, a mistake in judgment means a date with the grim reaper.

Wednesday through Saturday from 4 until the last person leaves. If you're traveling with a group touring the area, the owner will gladly open up early for you if you call a day or two ahead. How's that for motorcycle friendly!

At Mile 52, turn right on SR 176, also known as the **Little River Canyon Parkway.** A favorite of local motorcycle riders for years, the road runs along a deep narrow gorge carved over the centuries by the **Little River.** This highway has some of the most dramatic overlooks anywhere in the South. The road has received some bad reviews in the past because it sorely needed repaving, but in 2005 the surface was recoated and the road is now smooth as a baby's bottom. But, since the resurfacing, a few of the pull-off areas were poorly graded and still have 6 to 10 inch drop-offs from the road bed, so use caution. Hopefully, by the time this book hits the streets, Alabama DOT will have corrected that little oversight. There are a couple of areas just a few feet from the road where you can park and walk the 50 feet to a sheer 700-foot drop into the canyon below. No guard rails or restraints of any kind. Be careful! Definitely not for the acrophobic.

And here's something for you trivia buffs, there are approximately 142 curves in the 11 mile ride through the canyon (give or take a few).

Continue on 176 to **Dog Town** where it intersects with CR 81 at Mile 67 and continue onto CR 81. Ignore the road signs that want you to turn right on CR 89. At Mile 70.6, turn right on US 11 and head north 4.6 miles to SR 35,

Earthquake!

At 3:59 a.m. on April 29, 2003, residents in Mentone were jolted out of bed—literally—when a rare 4.9 magnitude earthquake erupted under the mountain. Thankfully, there were no fatalities but almost everyone you meet who lives in and around this area can tell you exactly what they did when the quake hit. Some thought it was a bomb or a gas tank exploding or an airplane crash. One little boy told CNN that he thought Jesus had come back. Few people realize it but the most damaging earthquake prior to the 1906 San Francisco event happened in Charleston in 1886 and was estimated at 7.3 on the Richter scale. The quake caused damage as far away as Atlanta, Georgia, and Richmond, Virginia. But don't worry about visiting. The southeast Tennessee seismic zone experiences one minor quake of this type every 20 years or so, and really doesn't expect a large quake anytime soon, according to geologists at Georgia Tech. ∎

Known as the Sock Capitol of the World, The Hosiery Museum located beside the Fort Payne Opera House is a must see historical attraction in this northeastern Alabama town.

which takes you into the **Sock Capitol of the World,** or known locally as **Ft. Payne,** Alabama. Ft. Payne's most famous residents, at least to country music fans, are the members of the group, **Alabama.** With a career that to date has resulted in 21 gold, platinum, and multi-platinum albums, 42 number one singles, and over 73 million records sold, this trio of Alabamians represents good ole southern values and traditions. Some would call them plain rednecks made good, and thankfully they're proud of it. While in Ft. Payne, check out the **Opera House** located on US 11 (510 North Gault Avenue, 256-845-3479). Next door is the Dekalb County Hosiery Museum (888-805-4740) which celebrates Ft. Payne's status as the "Sock Capitol of the World." Train buffs will want to visit the **Ft. Payne Depot Museum,** located at 105 5th Street Northeast, beside Union Park (256-845-5714). It is open Monday through Wednesday and on Friday 10 to 4 p.m., and on Sunday 2 to 4 p.m., other days by appointment (www.fortpaynedepotmuseum.org).

When you're ready, retrace your route to SR 35 and head west through the towns of **Rainsville** and **Section** along **Guntersville Lake** to return to Scottsboro and your starting point.

Trip 3 Mt. Cheaha Loop

Distance *107 miles*
Terrain *Pass over Mt. Cheaha, the highest point in Alabama and descend on a twisty mountain road through the Talladega National Forest before returning up the other side of the mountain*
Highlights *Scenic overlooks, tight twisties, and ghost stories*

This adventure begins in **Oxford,** Alabama, at US 78 and SR 21. I chose this intersection because there are plenty of affordable overnight lodgings available within a stone's throw of the interstate. Travel east on US 78 for 11.3 miles and turn left onto the access road. In .7 miles, you'll turn right onto SR 281, also known as **Skyway Mountainway.**

Immediately, you'll have entered a motorcyclist's dream highway as the twists and turns begin almost before you settle onto the highway. A bit of

Elevation changes and knee dragging curves make for a great combination on the Skyway Mountainway, a part of the Mt. Cheaha Loop ride!

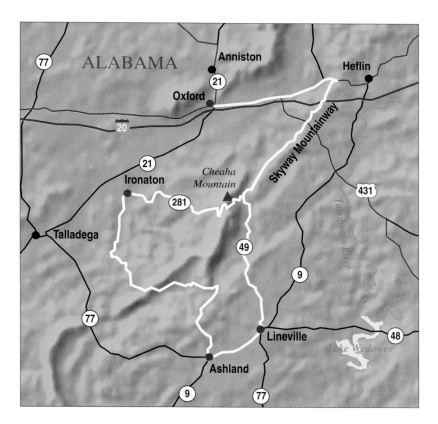

caution is called for on this initial section of the Skyway because of the presence of asphalt gravel. There isn't enough traffic to clear the loose impediments, so for the first few miles extreme leans in the tight corners might ruin this ride before it starts.

Soon after you cross the interstate you'll come to one of many pull-offs that will tempt you to stop and gaze at the gorgeous views spread out before you. You have an option. Stop and take in the view now, or continue on and stop on the return trip. Yes, that's right; I enjoyed this road so much that I'm going to bring you right back to it at the end of the ride.

There is no commercial development along this stretch of road but you will notice pickup trucks pulled off the road into the edge of the woods at various intervals. If you're not an outdoorsman, you might wonder what's going on. In the hunting season, these trucks belong to an important species that helps keep the **Talladega National Forest** deer population in check and known as *huntimus bambinimus,* or deer slayers. You'll recognize the species by its colors, dappled green and brown from head to toe with a bright orange chest and

It's a beautiful stretch of road that leads to nowhere. If you miss the turnoff while riding the Talladega Parkway you'll wind up on this section of highway that dead-ends about one mile later. If you see this view, you've gone too far!

back. The male and female of the species are indistinguishable in this habitat. You don't need to worry about the *huntimus bambinimus,* unless you're planning on hiking through their territory during periods of high activity. To protect yourself, make lots of noise and wear a bright orange suit.

In 18 miles, you'll reach the entrance to **Mt. Cheaha State Park,** (2141 Bunker Loop, Delta, 256-488-5115). In native Creek Indian dialect, Cheaha means "high place" and that's exactly what you'll find in this State Park which was constructed in the early '30s by the CCC (Civilian Conservation Corps). Turn right and, if you've a mind to, give the ranger a saw buck ($1) to enter the park proper and ride the 2.5 mile loop through the campground. If you do, stop in at Bunker Tower and climb to the top. Then you can truthfully boast that you've been to the highest point in Alabama (2,407 feet). At the **Doug Ghee Tail,** you'll find views that will have you digging around in you saddlebag for your digital camera.

If you're hungry at this point, you might check out the restaurant at the park. I can't recommend it for its food because every time I've eaten there it's been buffet style, but with the view you forget the food anyway.

When you've completed the loop, you'll arrive back at the general store. If you're lost or just turned around, the clerks in the store are most helpful, as they know the roads in this area even better than I. On my first visit, my map was slightly wrong, and when I dug it out to ask the clerk, she smiled politely and said, "You ain't from around here are you?" She was just joshing me, but since I had that lost puppy dog look, I guess I deserved it. That was the one time my Delorme Atlas and Gazetteer let me down, but that meant I found a new friend, and that's always a good thing.

Just a short distance past the State Park entrance, you'll see a sign that shows an arrow pointing right with a sign for Hwy 21.The map says this is Hwy 42. Neither myself nor the lady at the store, or even the local deputy sheriff, could explain that! All the locals know this road as Cheaha Road. The Deputy confessed that the road continued through four different counties so nobody refers to it by a highway number anyway. Someone should inform the folks at the Alabama Department of Road Signs. You'll need to turn right onto Cheaha Road to continue this adventure. If you miss this turn, you'll eventually come to the abrupt end of the Skyway Mountainway about ten miles later.

As a side trip, this is a pleasant way to spend 30 minutes or so. Since it's a well maintained highway to nowhere and only used by hikers, hunters, and lost motorcyclists, you'll enjoy twisting the throttle and leaning into the last few curves before the parking lot at the end.

THE ROUTE FROM OXFORD

0	Start on SR 21 and US 78 in Oxford
11.8	Turn left onto the access road for SR 281
12.0	Turn right onto SR 281
31.0	Entrance to Mt. Cheaha State Park
32.0	Turn right onto Cheaha Road
44.5	Turn left on McElderry Road
45.0	Turn left on Twin Churches Road
50.0	Turn left on Cemetery Mountain Road
54.0	Road name changes to Gunterstown Road
56.0	Turn left on Hanging Rock Road
57.0	Turn left on Clairmont Springs Road
63.4	Turn right on CR 31
71.5	Turn left on SR 9
77.3	Turn left on SR 49
91.5	Turn right on SR 281
107.0	End at Hwy 78 access road

Back on Cheaha Road, you'll pass **Cheaha Lake** at the bottom of the mountain and continue west through the **Talladega National Forest** for the next nine miles. In places the road isn't in the best condition as the annual freeze and thaw cycle does its best to return the land to a natural state, but that only means you shouldn't try to set a new road racing speed record on this stretch. Instead, settle for a moderate pace and you'll enjoy the road as it winds its way through sparsely populated stands of hardwood and southern pines.

At Mile 44.5, you'll turn left onto McElderry Road. Don't bother twisting that throttle too much because you'll turn left again onto Twin Churches Road (CR 385) in less than half a mile at Mile 45. This will carry you through the small community of **Ironaton** (pronounced I-roan-a-ton). Not that you'd have any reason to stop, but if you were talking to someone later about your travels, and mentioned this wide spot in the road by name, you would be in the company of a very small group of people if you used the correct pronunciation.

Just past Ironaton, at Mile 50, turn left onto Cemetery Mountain Road (CR 394). Honestly, these highway number references I'm giving you are useless in this part of Alabama! The signs are almost non-existent. Even the normal highway name signs are often missing. I don't know who is in charge of the tourism department in this part of Alabama, but they're not too keen on keeping us informed.

At Mile 54, you'll continue straight onto Gunterstown Road, although you won't notice any change. The road winds through the backwoods of Alabama and as you pass these humble dwellings your mind may start to wonder just how far it is to the nearest Starbucks, and how do these people survive way out here in the boonies.

At Mile 56.2, you'll turn left onto Clairmont Springs Road and without your knowledge, or any outward appearance, you will have just entered the twilight zone. Legend has it that this area is rife with ghosts. According to folklore, the ruins of the nearby **Clairmont Springs Hotel** is built on the site of an ancient Indian burial ground. Besides all the bad karma that poor planning brings, it is also supposed to be haunted by the ghost of a seven year old girl who was killed when she was struck by a train in 1972. The locals in nearby Ashland don't put much stock in the stories, but still, I wouldn't wander too much off the stated route, unless you're a certified card carrying Ghostbuster.

At Mile 63.5, turn right onto CR 31 and travel eight miles to the town of **Ashland.** Now, movie buffs might be inclined to assume that Ashland is the setting for the movie Big Fish based on the book by Daniel Wallace. It's a good movie, but the movie town of Ashland in the book is based on **Cullman,** Alabama, not Ashland, Alabama. The author says he saw an exit sign for Ashland, Virginia, and took that for the name, not realizing that 127 miles away from Cullman was a real Ashland, Alabama. Confused yet? Well, it gets better because that same author wrote another book in 2003 entitled *Watermelon King* and that book is based in Ashland, Alabama, only Ashland isn't known for raising watermelons; it's known for processing chickens with nearby **Tyson Foods** being a major employer. Now I'm thoroughly confused, but that's nothing new.

As you leave Ashland, turn left on to SR 77/9 and travel east. In a short five miles, you'll reach the town of **Lineville**, Alabama.

At Mile 88, turn left onto SR 49. In about 14 miles you'll return to SR 281 (Skyway Mountainway). Before you do, however, you'll enjoy miles of tight twisties across **Tater Mountain** that will delight even the most diehard knee dragging junkie.

At Mile 91, turn right onto SR 281. The next 16 miles should look familiar since you traveled this path about 90 miles ago. Now is the time to enjoy those pull-offs you rode past earlier, or if you've already taken in the scenery, then concentrate on the road and enjoy the twists and turns. Just remember the loose impediments after you cross over the interstate.

The South is rich in unspoiled areas to ride, just like the Talladega National Forest. This road was made for cruiser riders who love to throttle back and enjoy the view!

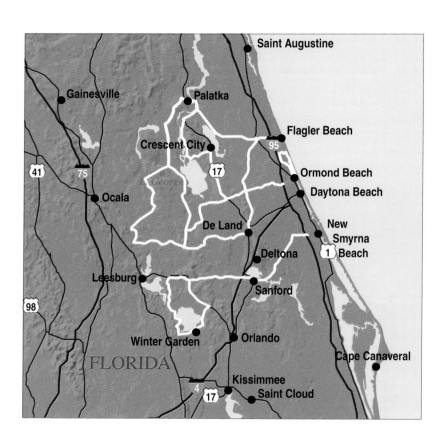

Escaping Bike Week Madness

Central Florida Getaways

Daytona sits smack in the middle of some of Florida's worst urban sprawl and at first blush there isn't much to recommend it to the touring-minded motorcycle traveler. However, in this book are a couple of good rides that will take you away from **Bike Week** and into the countryside where the traffic is somewhat lighter and the food beats traditional Bike Week fare. If you've never heard of these spots, don't feel bad. I'd been attending Daytona's Bike Week for most of a decade before I decided to leave the madness and explore, and I'm glad I did!

Once I hit the road, it wasn't long before I discovered **Palatka,** Florida (www.co.putnam.fl.us/palatka). The "gem" of the St. Johns River, Palatka makes for a short daytrip from Daytona. If you're looking for something longer, I've put together a couple of routes that take you through Palatka and into a few other charming central Florida towns.

Enjoy the beauty of this vanishing area of Florida while you can because the evidence of man's encroachment on nature can be seen more and more along this loop.

You'll find yourself wishing you could slow down the hands of time in Sanford, Florida, as you stroll this beautiful downtown square.

Overflowing with charm-appeal is **Sanford,** Florida, which we visit on our Florida Mountain tour. Yes, there are "mountains" in Florida and I'll take you to three of them. Actually two of them are just names of towns, **Mt. Dora** and **Mt. Plymouth,** but the third is an actual mountain on the highway maps of the state. **Sugarloaf Mountain** and the **Green Mountain Scenic Byway** are relatively unspoiled by urban growth but I've a feeling that won't last very long. After you pass through **Montverde,** you'll have a nice view of **Lake Apopka** on your left. If the oranges are ripe, you might swipe a few from the orange groves lining the highway; just don't fill up your saddlebags. If you want more than a couple, you can buy them at the roadside stands very cheap.

Another good route out of Bike Week runs west toward the town of **Barberville** and the **Pioneer Settlement** (www.pioneersettlement.org). The best time to visit the Settlement is during the **Fall Jamboree.** Held on the first weekend in November the Jamboree brings Florida's folk history and culture alive through demonstrations of turn-of-the-century backwoods life, folk, and domestic arts, and the cultural mix of people who have lived and settled the region. The Settlement is also open other times throughout the year.

Probably my favorite "Get out of Bike Week Tour," which I call "Hunting the Ma Barker Gang," will take most of a day but for me it's well worth it. The route takes you through **Crescent City** (www.crescentcityflorida.com) where you might hear tales of a local pirate who plied the waters of **Dunns Creek** and **Lake Crescent.** Local legend has it that **Jack the Ugly** stashed his pirate booty in these parts but I've never stumbled over it.

Mt. Dora is a good place to stop and stretch your legs during your "Mountains of Florida" tour.

But, it's the legend of the **Ma Barker Gang** that first got me out of Bike Week and over to the town of **Oklawaha.** This town, on the shores of **Lake Weir,** lays claim to being the site of the FBI's largest gun battle in history. Close to 4000 rounds of gunfire were exchanged between the G-Men and that infamous criminal Barker Gang. The irony of the whole thing is how an alligator was the unwitting accomplice of the Feds and helped them uncover their hideout.

For food, you'll want to stop in Palatka at **Angels Diner**, where you'll swear you stepped back half a century. In Crescent City you must try **The Three Bananas.** West of Barberville is **The Blackwater Inn** which overlooks the **St. Johns River,** and in Oklawaha is **Gator Joe's.** Gator Joe's is an obvious tourist-type eatery but it does have good food and you can learn all about how Gator Joe helped the Feds bring down Ma Barker and her gang.

You may notice that in this section of the book there aren't many listings for lodging. I'm assuming that many of you will, as I do, explore this region while staying in Daytona during one of the semi-annual motorcycle rallies and won't need lodging information. However, if historic bed-and-breakfast inns are your thing, there is the authentic Victorian **Higgins House** (www.higginshouse.com) in **Sanford,** with a room rate of $125 to $145 per night. I haven't actually stayed at the Sanford, but I have heard good comments and the owners are motorcycle-friendly. You might also check the **Shamrock**

There are several ways to ride the loop but my favorite is to end at this park at the intersection of John Anderson Drive and Granada.

This cupola is all that remains of the Ormand Hotel. Inside you'll probably find a volunteer to explain the historical photos lining the walls.

Thistle and Crown near **Lady Lake** at **Weirsdale,** which is close to the route. Call 800-425-2763 for reservations (www.shamrockbb.com).

So, the next time someone tries to tell you that Florida is flat and boring, you can dispute that with the confidence that comes from having ridden the Mountains of Florida, hunted the Ma Barker Gang, and dug for pirates' gold—all during one trip to Bike Week.

Trip 4   Ma Barker Gang and Big Jack the Ugly

Distance *177 miles*
Terrain *It's Florida, what do you expect? Mostly flat and straight except for a short stretch around mile 39. Traffic is moderate in the country, heavy in town.*
Highlights *Pioneer Village, Pirates in Cresent City, Gator Joe's. That's got to be more fun that duck-walking down Main Street, right?*

Every guidebook author knows that compiling the information for his or her book requires a fair bit of research. I like to approach each subject with an open mind, without preconceived ideas or prejudices about locales. That's why I was sure the history of Barberville just had to be linked to the barber profession. After all, 10.5 miles from this town lies the town of **Seville.** So that's where the Barber of Seville came from, right? Okay, quit moaning, it was lame, but what better segue than that to open this chapter with this little community that sits smack on the crossroads of the well traveled Hwy 17 and Rt. 40.

Who says you can't escape the madness of Bike Week and enjoy a good ride and great grub. Gator Joe's in Weirsdale provides the perfect excuse to explore a part of Florida you may never have heard about. (Photo by Sylvia Cochran)

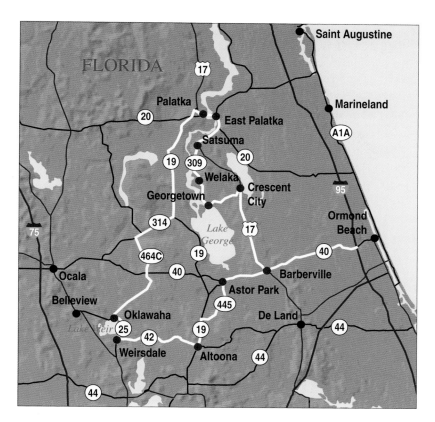

The town of **Barberville** was established in 1882 by **James D. Barber** who wasn't a barber by profession, but did possess the kind of entrepreneurial spirit that made America great. Because this area was on the proposed route of the **Jacksonville, Tampa, and Key West Railroad,** Barber gambled it would be the perfect spot to put down roots and stake his claim to posterity. He almost made it. History records that James D. Barber served as an agent for the J,T, & KW Railroad and later as an agent for the **Plant and Atlantic Coast Line Railroad.** However, the sands of time shifted progress away from Barberville toward the coast, and while the town didn't become the booming metropolis that Barber had envisioned, it does boast an eclectic roadside flea market for the person who loves kitsch, and a wonderful example of early Florida history at **The Pioneer Settlement for the Creative Arts.**

Open to the public, the Settlement showcases the lifestyle of Florida's early settlers with a tour that includes butter churning, spinning, candle dipping, and weaving. In addition there are outdoor displays of Florida's Native American tribes (Timucuan, Miccasuccee, and Seminoles) making pottery, tools,

THE ROUTE FROM BARBERVILLE

0	Start on SR 40 at I-95
19.7	Turn right on US 17
38.0	Turn right on Cypress Avenue to Three Banana's Landing
38.5	Turn left on US 17
39.0	Turn right on Junction Road
40.5	Turn left on Denver Road/Crescent City Road
40.7	Turn right on Georgetown Denver Road
46.9	Turn right on CR 309
61.5	Turn left on US 17 through Palatka
75.5	Turn left on CR 19
98.0	Turn right SR 314
109.0	Turn left on SR 314a
115.0	Go straight onto CR 464
127.8	Go straight onto 135 Avenue. Stop at Gator Joe's Restaurant.
128.0	Return to CR 25, and turn right
133.2	Turn left on CR 42
151.2	Turn left on CR 19
156.4	Turn right on CR 445
167.8	Turn right on SR 40 through the town of Astor Park
177.5	Arrive in Barberville

and bead work. Food history buffs will appreciate the lesson in making lassie cake. For the uneducated (of which I was once a member), lassie is slang for molasses, and a lassie cake is a cake made from—well, molasses. As we all know, molasses is the juice extracted from the sugarcane plant before being refined into the white bleached crystallized sugar we pick up in the supermarket. While the process has changed somewhat since the early settlers gathered each fall for 'cane grinding, the "Settlement" shows visitors what it was like in the days before there was a Super Wal-Mart to gather your winter foods.

As you leave Barberville you have a choice. Head north on Hwy 17, or explore the Old Hwy 17, now designated CR 3, and running roughly parallel on the west side of the railroad. The detour on Old 17/CR 3 isn't very long, but you will experience a more leisurely pace for 7.4 miles, until it rejoins Hwy 17. CR 3 winds through several residential sections and the speed limit slows to 35 mph, so if you're in a hurry you might stick to the more modern Hwy 17; but

Simple Lassie Cake Recipe

2 1/2 cups molasses
2 cups boiling water
2 1/2 tsp. baking soda
8 tbsp. Crisco or lard or your choice
2 tbsp. ginger
1 egg, beaten slightly
6 cups of flour

Mix all ingredients in order given. Put into greased and floured pan. Bake in preheated, 375 degree oven for 50 minutes. Cool slightly before removing cake from pan. Serve warm or cold.

Years ago, some cooks would substitute 2 cups of strong black coffee for the water. This gave the molasses cake a "kick" and a different flavor, as you can imagine. ∎

A few hundred yards from this spot in Lake Crescent, lies the wreck of the Black Swan, scuttled by the pirate known as Big Jack the Ugly.

Abundant sunshine and motorcycle friendly destinations are plentiful in central Florida. Bring your sunglasses and take my advice, always wear sunscreen, SPF 50 if possible.

this short scenic section is blessed with several miles of live oaks towering over palm trees and is a welcome respite to the quickened pace just several hundred yards off to your right. In places you can glimpse the cars whizzing by on the parallel road and those of you with a philosophical bent will no doubt appreciate the break, however slight, from life's frenetic pace. To ride CR 3, go two tenths of a mile west on Hwy 17 from the intersection of Route 40 and turn left.

Either route you choose, our next stop is in Crescent City.

At Mile 38, you'll turn right at the only stoplight in **Crescent City** onto Central Avenue which ends a half mile later at **Crescent Lake** and the **Three Bananas Landing.** It just so happens that there's also a restaurant called the **Three Bananas** right on the water at this location (www.3bananas.com). Three Bananas is open every day except Tuesday, but be warned, they don't take checks or credit cards. The house specialty is the Sliced Jerk Chicken, but I like Jerry's Belly Bustin Blue Cheese Burger. If you arrive in early April, the locals put on a **Catfish Festival** which has the requisite arts and crafts, car show and parade, and of course, fried fish, straight from the local catfish ponds.

Besides catfish, Crescent City is also known for its pirates. No, not the modern kind, but the big hat, eye patch, stuff of legends and myths. The townsfolk claim that in the 1700s, seafaring pirates would hide out in Crescent

Lake, making provisions and repairing their vessels, safe from the authorities who patrolled St. Augustine and Charleston. These legends may have their origins in the tale of **Big Jack the Ugly** (what a great name for a pirate rogue huh?), who captured the frigate *The Black Swan,* sailed it to Crescent Lake, stripped it of everything of value, and scuttled it 2500 yards south of Three Bananas landing. Divers report finding parts of *The Black Swan* beneath the blue waters, and the locals swear that Big Jack the Ugly buried his treasure around the shores of Crescent City amongst the large cypress trees. What a time to forget my folding army shovel. Where's the nearest hardware store?

After taking in your fill of the lake and the food at Three Bananas, return to US 17, and retrace your route to Highway 17. Turn left and head back south .7 miles to Junction Road (19.4 miles) where you'll turn right heading west toward another large body of inland water, **Lake George.** 1.5 miles later, Junction Road ends at Union Avenue and you'll turn left for .1 mile and turn back right on Georgetown Denver Road.

Georgetown Denver Road is a little out of the way, but after the dull straight Hwy 17, you'll appreciate the curves along this route. The signs change from Georgetown Denver Road to Crescent City Road, but it's all the same road and you remain on this route for seven miles.

A popular gathering place for two wheel tourists and locals alike, the Three Bananas also serves as a prime spot to view the Space Shuttle launch. No kidding!

When you reach CR 309 (Mile 27), turn right into **Georgetown** and travel north. The lake here is off to your left and if you're interested in taking in the view, you can reach it via one of the access roads which branch off CR 309. This section of road isn't very well maintained so be alert to any potential trouble spots. During certain times of the year you may see what appears to be discarded gallon milk jugs in the water-filled ditch. However, if you notice their placement at regular intervals, you may soon realize these are homemade buoys marking the location of mudpuppy traps. Mudpuppies are also known as Crawfish, or Crayfish. I'm sure you've seen the little red 4 to 6 inch long crustaceans which are distant cousins to the lobster. My wife hates it when I order them; she says I'm eating bugs. I see it as true southern culture, at least all the culture I'm interested in.

In about a mile and a half, turn right to stay on CR 309 as it intersects with Lake George Point Drive. After a short stretch (.2 of a mile) stay on CR 309 as it bends left, and follow this into the town of **Welaka**. If you have time, you could pause at the **Welaka National Fish Hatchery.** Open 7 to 4 p.m. daily, the hatchery raises between 4.5 to 5 million fish annually. Species vital to the fishery resources of Florida, Georgia, Alabama, and the coastal United States are raised here and stocked in cooperation with the various state game and fish agencies. Unless they've changed the rules, they don't allow shooting the fish in the barrel, but it's a nice diversion to stretch your legs.

At the Ft. Gate Ferry road you have a choice. If you're an accomplished rider and want to bypass Palatka to try your hand at something really unique, turn left and ride one mile to the **Ft. Gates Ferry.** Established in 1856, the ferry is a small flat barge powered by a diesel tugboat. You can pull your motorcycle right on the ferry/barge for a 15 to 20 minute ride across the **St. Johns River.** Once on the western shore you are disgorged onto a road with the designation FR 43. Don't bother to look for it on most maps as you'll need a Delorme Atlas (which I recommend for you power touring commandos) to find it. From there it's about seven miles of gravel road to **Salt Springs,** and pavement. This route isn't for the beginning rider or someone on a large touring bike, but anyone with experience riding off-road bikes or those riding dual sport bikes won't have any trouble! Once in Salt Springs, you can turn north on CR 19 and pick up the route we're taking at SR 314.

After Ft. Gates Ferry Road you enter the **Welaka State Forest** and you'll pick up US 17 again at **Satsuma** where CR 309 merges with US 17 for a spell. Turn left onto US 17, and head north, and about three miles later you'll cross the high bridge at **Dunns Creek,** which feeds Lake Crescent from the St. Johns River. It's easy to believe that in the 1700s this would have been a haven for pirates sailing to winter hideouts in Lake Crescent.

First it was occupied by the Native Americans, then came the Spanish, next the English and their tea, and now bikers and tourists flock to this Land between the lakes!

A few miles later as you enter **East Palatka,** you'll pass the **Cheyenne Saloon,** motorcycle friendly year-round and especially during Bike Week. On this trip we continue through Palatka. For a more detailed description of this historic town, see page 73.

Turn left on 9th Street/Hwy 20 which 2.2 miles later will meet Hwy 19. Turn right on 19 heading south out of town and 10 miles later you'll enter the **Ocala National Forest.** Turn right on SR 314. For the next 20 miles or so, except for the occasional car you meet and the paved highway you're riding on, this could be Florida as it was when the first Europeans landed on its beaches searching for gold or the fountain of youth. Ok—the slash pine and sago palm might not be native, but that's splitting hairs. If you enjoy solitude, this stretch of road is almost heaven.

Turn left onto Rt 464C and continue south toward the town of **Oklawaha** (pronounced "ahk-lah-wah-ah"). Along the road you'll notice huge 5 to 6-foot nests at the tops of tall poles, which I believe are bald eagle nests. I didn't actually see an eagle but then again I didn't camp out long enough to wait for one to land.

GATOR JOE'S FOOT

JOE WAS A 15 FT. 7 IN. ALLIGATOR THAT LIVED ON LAKE WEIR IN THE EARLY 1900's. HE CAUGHT HIS FAME FROM THE MA BARKER GANG, WHO TRIED TO KILL HIM ON SEVERAL OCCASIONS; BUT JOE ULTIMATELY GOT THEM INSTEAD. HIS LOCAL LEGEND LED THE F.B.I. TO THE BARKER HIDEOUT ON JANUARY 16, 1935 AND AFTER A 4-HOUR GUN BATTLE THE GANG ALL LAY DEAD. IN 1952 JOE CROSSED PATHS WITH A LOCAL GATOR HUNTER NAMED VIC SKIDMORE. SINCE THEN JOE'S FOOT HAS HAD MANY HOMES THROUGH OUT FLORIDA AND EVEN IN KENTUCKY. IT WAS DONATED TO US FROM ONE OF VIC'S FRIENDS MR. JIM TOWNSLEE.

ON LOAN From The Lake Weir Chamber

The shootout with the Ma Barker Gang stands as the largest gun battle in history. Here you can read about the legend of Gator Joe and how he helped the FBI locate this infamous gang.

In Oklawaha, Route 464C ends at CR 25. Oklawaha lays claim as the site of the FBI's largest gun battle in history. On January 16, 1935, in a four hour period, 3000 to 4000 rounds of ammo were exchanged between the Ma Barker Gang and agents of the FBI. Each January the townsfolk reenact the shootout with the only difference being nobody actually dies. Continue straight where Route 464C ends onto 135th Avenue. At the lake, stop in at **Gator Joe's Beach Bar and Grill** (12431 135th Avenue, www.gatorjoes.biz, 352-288-3100). Here you'll find lots of memorabilia and folklore about Gator Joe, the 15-foot gator that snitched to the FBI and helped them locate the fugitives. Besides the Ma Barker memorabilia, Gator Joe's rafters are hand lettered with sayings such as "Did you eat a bowl of stupid this morning," "I will always cherish the initial misconception I had about you," and my favorite, "I'm not bald, I'm too tall for hair." By now, you should be able to tell that Gator Joe's isn't a wine and cheese establishment (although they do serve the standard white and red $10 bottles.) The food is good, the atmosphere is all beach bum, and no—they won't turn down the music.

If you're in the mood for some grub, try my favorite appetizer on their menu, the Key West Conch Fritters. But, if you're really hungry, the Captains Combo is the way to go. For as much money as you throw at the cook, you can have a platter piled with fried shrimp, clams, fish plank, frog legs, and gator tail.

Pithy sayings help pass the time as you wait on your Conch Fritters or the Gator Philly Sandwich, made with, you guessed it, alligator meat.

After you've eaten your fill, you'll pick up Route 25 and head south around the east side of **Lake Weir** to the intersection of Hwy 42 in Weirsdale. Turn left on Hwy 42 heading east. At **Altoona** turn north onto Rt. 19 to CR 445. Turn Right on CR 445 heading through the interior of the Ocala National Forest. While not technically challenging, this is a quiet and peaceful ride through natural sand ridges. CR 445 merges with CR 445A for a short distance where it ends at Route 40. Turn left and head toward Barberville. At the drawbridge to cross the St. Johns River is the **Blackwater Inn.** If you've skipped all the other eating locations, The Blackwater Inn overlooking the "river that flows north" is a favorite among locals with reasonable priced, well-prepared food.

After crossing the river you'll soon arrive back at your starting point of Barberville.

Trip 5 Riding Florida's Mountains

Distance *107 miles*

Highlights *An honest to goodness elevation change in Florida! A few miles of twisty two lanes and quaint and charming Florida towns with fresh oranges (in season).*

Terrain *The Green Mountain Scenic Byway will, for a few miles, allow you to forget you're in Florida. Traffic is heavy to congested in the cities depending on the day and time. Avoid rush hours. I have tried to keep you off the heaviest traveled roads, but for the most part this is unavoidable.*

Also known as the Green Mountain Byway, CR 455 leads you to Montverde, a town with beautiful architecture and an interesting history. (Photo by Sylvia Cochran)

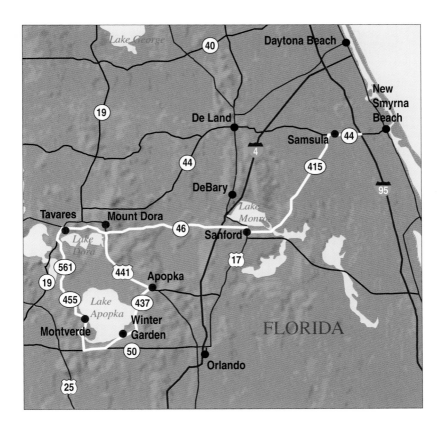

I'd be willing to bet you a dollar to a donut that you thought Florida was completely flat, and admittedly so did I. In fact, I once commented in an editorial that the State is flatter than my Grandma's lacy cornbread. For the most part that's true, yet I can take you on a journey that will give you a "one-up" on even some of the locals!

Sometimes you ride for the great roads, other times you ride for a memorable destination, and then sometimes you ride a road or to a destination just because you want to be able to say you did it.

This is one of those times. In any other state in these United States, this ride wouldn't rate an honorable mention, but the look on people's faces when you tell them you rode the only mountain in Florida is—well, almost priceless.

I remember being in a party in Daytona during Bike Week and a real windbag was going on and on about riding his bike through the mountains of some Third World country. Someone asked me If I'd ever ridden anywhere exciting like that and I made the statement, "I've ridden the only mountain in Florida!"

THE ROUTE FROM DAYTONA BEACH

0   SR 44 at I-95, head west
4.6   Left on CR 415
22.1   Right to stay on CR 415
25.9   Right on US 17
26.7   Right on 1st Street and retrace route to US 17/SR 46
27.2   Straight on SR 46
49.2   Straight on 1st Avenue
49.8   Right on North Highlands
50.4   Left on East 11th Street
51.6   Straight onto Helm Street/Old US 441
55.0   Straight onto Alfred Street
56.4   Bear right on Lake Shore Boulevard
56.6   Left on SR 19
58.3   Left on CR 561
67.0   Left on CR 455 (Green Mountain Scenic Byway)
78.6   Left on SR 50
80.5   Left on SR 438
87.3   Left on CR 437 (Ocoee Apopka Road)
95.2   Left on CR 435 South Park Avenue
95.5   Left on US 441
107.0   Right onto CR 46

The look of disbelief on Mr. Bag-O-Wind was a "Kodak moment." "What mountain?" was the reply and playing the jester I couldn't resist. "You mean you've lived in Florida all your life and you've never ridden Sugarloaf Mountain?" I wasn't sure if his upturned nose and raised eyebrow meant he regarded me as a raving lunatic or a bald-faced liar. I was stretching the truth a bit, because there are actually two high spots that carry the "mountains" designation in Florida. The other is Iron Mountain. Neither is the highest point in the state as that honor goes to Britton Hill near the Alabama line in the Panhandle section of the state; but Sugarloaf Mountain is the highest on the peninsula and the most "motorcycle friendly."

Since many of you visit Florida only once or twice a year and usually during the motorcycle rallies in Daytona, we'll start our journey at the intersection of US 44 and I-95, just south of Daytona Beach. Start out heading west on US 44 toward **Samsula.** Bike Week veterans know this area as home to Spotnik's Cabbage Patch, located on Tomoka Farms Road. **Spotnik's Cabbage Patch** hosts the World Famous Coleslaw Wrestling every Bike Week on Wednesday. It's so popular that the roads leading into the campground become jam-packed for several hours before the event starts. While coleslaw wrestling isn't an Olympic sport, I'm proud to say that my town, **Swainsboro,** Georgia, is home to a three-time winner of this event, and no, it's not me!

At SR 415 turn left and head south toward **Sanford.** At Mile 22.6, you have the option to take a short detour and turn right onto Chickasaw Drive. In a couple hundred feet you'll come to an **Indian shell mound** on the righthand side of the road. It isn't much to look at, but I mention it because it's an excellent example of a little known part of Florida's history. Indian shell mounds were the Native American's landfill. These shells, sometimes piled twenty feet high or more, were the leftovers of the shellfish eaten by the natives and piled higher and higher until abandoned. They can be found in other parts of the State as well. There's a sign warning you not to dig around in this historic waste dump!

You probably won't feel your ears pop from the changes in elevation as you ride Sugarloaf Mountain, but you will enjoy the change from the straight flat roads that you had to ride to get here. (Photo by Sylvia Cochran)

In the towns of central Florida the tourists take shopping seriously and they scarcely notice leather-clad, tattooed bikers.

Returning to Route 415, head west toward town. At the intersection of US 17 turn right for just under a mile until the intersection of SR 46/17 and First Street. If you're hungry, turn right on First Street and head into historic downtown. Sanford is located on the southern shores of **Lake Monroe** and is listed in the **National Register of Historic Places.** Sanford was once the largest vegetable shipping centers in the U.S., earning it the nickname of the "Celery City." Today the only celery you'll find is at **Rubyjuice Smoothies** on the corner of West First Street and North Park Avenue (407-322-3779). Rubyjuice was voted "Best Smoothie in Seminole County" according to the plaque on the wall. Since I haven't tried the other smoothie joints in the county I can't dispute that, but I know you can have almost any flavor smoothie you can imagine in this one, plus a few you've probably never even dreamed about. My favorite is the Peachy Keen, but I'm trying to get enough nerve to try the one made from saw grass. Yes, you read that right, grass. It's grown right in the store under grow lamps and it's supposed to cure whatever ails you.

If you're in need of more sustenance than a fruit (or grass) smoothie, try the **Blue Dahlia** (112 East 1st Street, 407-688-4745, www.bluedahlia-sanford.com). There's a scene from the movie *My Girl* in which Dan Akroyd is seated at the front window of this restaurant. Seating is also available outside. For good German food try the **Willow Tree Cafe** (205 East 1st Street, 407-321-2204, www.willowtreecafe.com).

When you've had your fill of downtown Sanford, head back west on First Street to the intersection of Routes 17 and 46. Continue west on 46 toward the first two "mountains" on this journey, Mount Plymouth and Mount Dora.

There's something special about Live Oak trees dripping with Spanish Moss which carries me back to my childhood and lazy summer days in the rural South. (Photo by Sylvia Cochran)

Spanish Moss and Live Oak Trees—
The Romance of the South

Native Americans called it "tree hair" and when our country was young it was routinely boiled as tea and used as treatments for rheumatism, abscesses, and birth pains. Legend has it that Henry Ford used it to stuff the seats in his first Model Ts but I can't confirm that. When I was growing up we always avoided it because we believed it contained chiggers, those nasty little bugs that you can't see but cause a rash of itching and red swollen skin. It is *Tillandsia Usneoides,* or Spanish Moss, and it is unique to the South. This grayish silver plant ranges from Virginia to Argentina. Technically, it's not a true moss and is actually in the same family as the pineapple. Don't ask me how botanists arrive at their classifications because I'll never understand. Contrary to myth, Spanish Moss is not a parasite and does not rob nutrients from its hosts. Instead, it gathers water and nutrients from the air directly through its own stems and leaves. Spanish Moss uses its host tree only for support, and interestingly enough will only grow in trees, not on fences or any other type of support. When I replay scenes from my youth, they always include images of massive 40 foot tall Live Oak trees, their branches heavy with long strands of Spanish Moss casting a 100 foot swath of shade.

The Live Oak tree is another instantly recognized symbol of the region. With a lifespan measured in centuries, the Live Oak has captured the imagination of southern poets and songwriters since this country was formed. When I was a child, I nailed a couple of boards between the branches of a live oak in my parents backyard for a makeshift tree house and often napped there during hot summer days. Once, I dozed late into the evening and missed supper. This caused a panic in my house and my parents alerted the neighborhood and soon everyone started looking for me. Finally someone thought to ask my older brother where he would look for me and he led them to that oak where I was found, still asleep. Until I became a parent I never fully understood what the fuss was about. If you've seen the movies *Gone With The Wind* or *Forrest Gump,* you get a sense of how these trees are woven into the very fabric of our lives here in the American South.   ∎

For the next 22 miles you'll pass by the **Seminole State Forest,** and you'll see "bear crossing" signs. Now I don't know about you but the prospect of hitting a bear at highway speed is enough to put me on high alert. I can ride though deer country secure in the knowledge that in an encounter with a deer my odds of survival are left to fate. With a bear it's a little more dicey because what happens if you only graze him and ruin his day! The thought of accidentally hitting a bear and then having him mad at me while I'm laying there with a broken leg is a little disconcerting, so I keep both eyes peeled for Yogi and Smokey.

Soon Route 46 will cross US 441 and dead end at Highland Street. Turn right and travel a couple of blocks to East 5th Street. Then turn left. This will take you through downtown **Mount Dora,** another quaint central Florida town filled with antiques and ambiance. If you're in a mood to try something really different, rent one of the Segways from **Segway of Central Florida** (140 West 5th Avenue, 352-383-9900). At $40 per hour or $10 for 10 minutes, you can see Mount Dora from a whole new perspective.

Fifth Avenue turns into Old US Hwy 441 and continues west along **Lake Dora** toward the town of **Tavares.** About this time the dense traffic will have you questioning my logic, but it's an unavoidable part of the ride. Just watch your Ps and Qs and you'll be fine. Soon old 441 turns into East Alfred Street, which turns into West Alfred Street. At Mile 56.6, you'll need to turn left on SR 19 and at Mile 58, left on CR 561.

It's easy to understand why retirees flock to Florida after you visit quaint towns like Winter Garden. With its clean and tidy streets, the downtown area just seems to encourage you to relax and enjoy a slower pace.

We Didn't Invent Moonshine, We Just Made It Famous

It was around long before Prohibition and known by many names, White Mule, Skat, Stump Juice, Mountain Dew, Fire Water, Rot Gut, and simply Shine. Yes, I have tasted moonshine, and yes, I have made moonshine, and yes, I have a recipe for making it that I can share with you. However, moonshine did not start in the South; that's a Hollywood myth. Actually, **Garrett,** Pennsylvania, had the distinction of being referred to as Moonshine, USA, during the depression. In fact, the first state to threaten to secede from the Union wasn't in the South and it wasn't during the Civil War. It was Pennsylvania, and it happened during the Whiskey Rebellion of 1794 when George Washington instituted a tariff on all homemade whiskey, a/k/a moonshine. This wasn't the only reason for the rebellion, but it was the proverbial straw that broke the camel's back. What moonshine did do for the South was cause the birth of stock car racing, known today as NASCAR. Many of these early stock car legends ran shine on Friday and Saturday nights and raced each other on Sunday. Oh, about that recipe, you'll have to email me for it: editor@usridernews.com. ∎

It's at this junction where I think the highest point in Florida is. No disrespect to the locals but if you look to your right, you'll spot a very tall hill with a couple of pieces of earth moving equipment on top. This is the county landfill. They wouldn't tell me how tall it is because of a silly Homeland Security restriction, but believe me, it's tall.

Continue on CR 561 south and you may begin to notice a stray cyclist or two. This area is well known to bicyclists who use the area to train. Now I'm not talking about the Schwinn banana-seat-casual Sunday afternoon rider. I'm talking spandex, funny helmet, "I could kick Lance Armstrong's butt if I had the chance" Tour De Wherever cyclist. Since hills are as rare in Florida as moonshiners in Manhattan, the area attracts bicyclists, motorcyclists, and sports car buffs so it hardly qualifies as the "Road Less Traveled."

At Mile 67, turn left onto CR 455, officially designated as the **Green Mountain Scenic Byway.** This road winds and twists among the hills of the area geologists call the **Lake Wales Ridge,** and roughly follows the contours of **Lake Apopka** along its western and southern shores. There are a couple of spots where you can catch a good view of the lake and at night you can even see the skyline of nearby **Orlando.**

This twisty section of road is only 12.5 miles long, and ends well before you tire of it. At Mile 73.1, you'll enter the last of our "mountain" towns, **Montverde**. In case you were wondering, Montverde means "green mountain" which is why my friends at Florida's DOT designated CR 455 as the Green Mountain Scenic Byway. The first thing you'll notice when you enter the town is the Mediterranean Revival style buildings of the 125-acre campus of Montverde Academy. CR 455 carries you straight through the campus and just past the southern entrance is Morningside Drive, a nice spot to pull over and stop for a good view of Lake Apopka.

CR 455 dead ends into Old Hwy 50 at Mile 78.6. Turn left and in 1.9 miles turn left again on CR 438. At Mile 82, you'll know you're approaching the town of **Winter Garden** as you pass under a canopy of moss-draped Live Oaks which completely cover the highway. I love riding the roads that pass under gnarled and twisted outstretched limbs of the great Live Oaks. They impart a mystical and almost foreboding feeling. Yet for all it portends, the feeling is familiar and comforting to this Son of the South who spent his childhood playing and digging in the dirt among the roots and the shadows of Live Oak trees very similar to these.

Soon the asphalt gives way to brick pavers as you enter the downtown area of Winter Garden. Vintage charm is the first phrase that comes to mind. Also, take notice of how clean and tidy this town is. If the renovations are complete and you have time to visit the **Garden Theater** on your right at 160 West Plant Street, stop in and see the crown jewel of this historic central Florida town. Train buffs will want to visit the **Central Florida Train Museum** (101 South Boyd Street, 407-656-0559) open daily from 1 to 5 p.m. with no charge for admission. Inside you'll find an excellent display of railroad china and a restored caboose, my favorite!

Leaving Winter Garden at Mile 86, turn left on CR 437 or Ocoee Apopka Road. If you're in a hurry, jump on SR 429 and head north to Apopka where 429 dead ends into US 441. Turn left and head back to Mt. Dora. If you stay on CR 437 however, turn left at Mile 95.2 on South Park Avenue for .3 mile to US 441. Then make the turn to Mt. Dora.

At Mile 107, our journey ends at the off ramp to CR 46. Turn right to retrace your route to I-4 in Sanford where you can hop on and head straight back toward Daytona and Bike Week madness.

Trip 6 Barberville, Palatka, and Ocala State Forest

Distance *147 miles*
Terrain *Mostly flat with farm country, national forests, pine thickets, and orange orchids. All roads are paved. Traffic is light to moderate in the country, and moderate in town.*
Highlights *Lakes, orange orchids, bald cypress trees, Florida Ghost towns, St. Johns River*

Daytona Bike Week attracts several hundred thousand motorcycle enthusiasts each year with the lure of warm weather, parties, and motorcycle racing. However, touring the countryside around Daytona isn't talked about much. Maybe that's because Florida isn't well known for having twisty challenging roads like the other major rally towns of Sturgis, South Dakota, or Laconia, New Hampshire.

The Ocala National Forest is the perfect spot to get away from the Daytona madness, but keep your eyes peeled for the occasional black bear crossing the road.

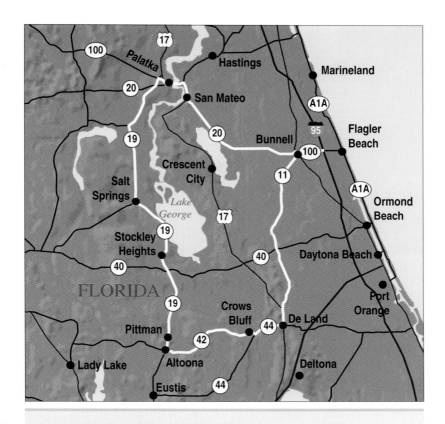

THE ROUTE FROM FLAGLER BEACH

0	Start on CR100 at I-95
4.6	Go straight onto SR 11 in the town of Bunnell
22.9	Go straight across SR 40. Stay on SR 11
34.5	Merge with US 17 and continue south
37.3	Turn right on SR 44 (West New York Avenue)
42.8	Turn right on SR 42
62.0	Turn right on SR 19, and approximately two miles later enter Ocala National Forest
114.3	Turn right on SR 20 (Crill Avenue). Follow SR 20 road signs. You will bear left once
117.0	Turn right on 17/100 and stop at Angels Diner on right
124.0	Turn left on 100/20 in San Mateo
147.0	Arrive in Bunnell on US 1

Kitschy is the only adjective appropriate for this roadside attraction but that's okay, because I've been known to give into my undiscriminating tastes and spend hours wandering through this flea market/fruit stand in Barberville. My advice, leave the buffalo but definitely buy the peanuts!

However, let's not dismiss central Florida so quickly. While there are few twisties to challenge the sport bike rider, there are a couple of country roads that allow you to lean a bit, and several historic and interesting destinations just waiting for you to discover.

We start our ride north of Daytona near Flagler Beach on East Moody Boulevard, CR 100. When you enter the town of **Bunnell** stay straight but pick up SR 11. For the next 18 miles you'll ride through the peaceful farming and ranching communities of Flagler and Volusia Counties. I often use this road as a quick "get out of town" detour loop from the craziness of Daytona Bike Week. Today we're going to take a much longer ride so at Mile 22.8, cross SR 40 and continue straight south.

Traffic along this stretch is moderate but still lighter than in the cities. This is the **Tomoka Wildlife Management Area** and development is mercifully sparse until you merge with Hwy 17 some 13 miles later. Still heading south the road turns into four lanes again, with more traffic as you approach **Deland**. If you have time you might want to detour the ride long enough to tour downtown Deland and visit the historic **Athens Theatre** and the **Volusia County Courthouse** both built in the 1920s. The courthouse is considered by many (at least in Deland) to be the most beautiful in the state. Deland is also home to Florida's first private university, Stetson University, founded as Deland Academy in 1883 by New York entrepreneur Henry Deland who believed that the town could be better promoted as a settlement if it boasted an educational institution. DeLand experienced financial difficulties in the middle 1880s as the result of a freeze and found it impossible to continue support for the university. He turned to his friend, **John Batterson Stetson,** the wealthy hat manufacturer and philanthropist for help with school funding. In 1887 Stetson was elected to the university board of trustees, and in 1889 the name of the university was changed to **John B. Stetson University.**

Turn right on Fla 44 (New York Avenue) and again at SR 42 to reach the town of **Crows Bluff,** one of the last remaining Ghost Towns of Florida. In the early 1800s Crows Bluff was an important river town which catered to the steamboat traffic. By the mid to late 1800s the railroad began taking the freight business away from steamboats and the river towns along the St. Johns began to dry up.

As you continue along Route 42, you'll pass several working dairy farms. For someone raised in the country, the odor of rotting silage is noticeable but not tremendously offensive. City folk might have a different opinion. To the uneducated, manure would be blamed for the odor, but trust me on this, organic fermentation is causing the stench. In case you needed to know, silage is corn leaves and/or root crops which are finely chopped and sliced, then mixed with fine ingredients such as spent grain and poultry litter, wetted thoroughly and covered tightly. After a few weeks, hardworking bacteria will have reduced the pile to something that cows seem to love, but motorcyclists hate to smell. In either case you can't hold your breath long enough to pass through so you might as well accept it. Concentrate on the good riding and block out the smell.

Sarsaparilla anyone? I was disappointed when I discovered this interesting building in Altoona, Florida, only sold items related to wells and well drilling, as I was really thirsty. Of course the sign out front should have given me a clue. (Photo by Sylvia Cochran)

In **Altoona** pick up Hwy 19 and head north through the towns of **Pittman** and **Stockley Heights** into the **Ocala National Forest.** If you're low on fuel, I recommend filling up in Altoona. The next gas stop is Salt Springs, some 30 miles north through the heart of the forest along the edge of Lake St. George.

For the next 14 miles we are warned to watch for bears. When most people think of Florida they naturally think of alligators and while the state has the highest population of these reptiles, they don't pose quite the threat to motorcyclists that bear or deer do. More than 50 of the estimated 2,000 Florida black bear are killed on Florida's roads each year. You may not see either bear or deer, but it's wise to keep a watchful eye.

Traffic is pleasantly light through the Ocala National Forest. The tall pine trees shade the late afternoon sun and it is easy to forget that you're only a few miles from the hustle and bustle of Bike Week. It is a welcome distraction.

All through the park, dirt roads branching off either side beckon the dual sport rider to take a detour into the interior of the park's 383,573 acres. The park has hundreds of camping sites, some full service while others are more rustic in nature. If you're interested, there is a wealth of information on the Ocala National Forest on the internet. Go to your favorite search engine and spend a couple of hours researching your trip here.

Getting out of town during Bike Week for a lazy afternoon doesn't take a lot of planning. You'll be surprised at the all the hidden jewels in central Florida waiting for you to discover!

The history of Palatka can be found painted on the sides of downtown buildings. Before he became known all over the world, a young Billy Graham was baptized and ordained as a minister of the gospels here.

Almost without warning the town of **Salt Springs** appears. Check your gas gauge and fill up if necessary. From Salt Springs we head north toward Palatka. When you reach Rt. 20, turn right and head into the town of Palatka.

In the northernmost edge of central Florida, the town of **Palatka** is rich in history. First settled by the Native Americans, the Spanish and English both claimed the land prior to Florida being turned over to America. In the 1600s the Spanish used it as a ranching area to feed the settlers in the St. Augustine area. In the mid 1700s the English crown took possession of Florida and pretty much ran the Spanish out of town. In 1774, the famous botanist William Bartram (the same guy who made that trail from the Appalachian mountains to Florida), visited the area and discovered the remains of a Native American village, on what was present day Palatka.

In 1835, the Seminoles attacked and burned Palatka and the settlers fled to St. Augustine. But a few years later the settlers returned and the natives were banished to history.

During the Civil War, Florida sat, for the most part, on the sidelines as there were no epic battles waged in the state. But, Civil War buffs will point out two interesting facts. The first is that **Tallahassee** was the only state capitol never to be occupied by the Union Army during the conflict. The second is that the only Cavalry capture in history of a naval vessel occurred in Florida when C.S.A. Cavalry Captain **J.J. Dickison**, nicknamed "Dixie" and "The Swamp Fox" took the Union gunboat *Columbine* at **Horse Landing** near Palatka.

While in town be sure to visit **Ravines Garden State Park.** Located on Twiggs Street right off Hwy 17, these gardens are beautiful during azalea season which happens to start in March, right around Bike Week. The landscape of the park was created over a period of thousands of years, by water flowing from the sandy ridges on the shore of the St. Johns River. In 1933, the resulting ravine was transformed into a garden by the **Federal Works Progress Administration.**

At the intersection of Routes 20 and 17S and at 100.3 miles, turn right and in roughly six tenths of a mile, you'll spot **Angels Dining Car** (209 Reid Street, Hwy 17/SR 100, 386-325-3927).

It looks just like the old diners of the 1930s, which is a good thing since it was founded by **Porter Angel** in 1932. Located within shouting distance of the St. Johns River, diners take a seat in the silver dining car in a pink and white decor, among old records and other antique memorabilia. If you're feeling adventurous, try the Black Bottom Burger, which is a scrambled egg, hamburger, and bacon burger that the locals swear by. For the traditionalist, Angels homemade hamburger (without the scrambled egg mixture) is so tender it will just about fall apart at the slightest provocation. The menu also lists nostalgic drinks such as Cherry Cokes and one called a Pusalow. Pronounced phew-salow, the drink hearkens to an earlier time when Saturday nights were spent in

The carhops don't wear bobby socks or tight sweaters but the food is good at Angels Diner, which lays claim as the oldest diner in Florida.

No, it's not a ramp, it's the Whitehair Drawbridge on the St. Johns River which flows south to north for 275 miles. Here's a trivia question most people miss: how many rivers in the USA flow south to north? Answer: At least nineteen, not counting the rivers that flow in a northwesterly direction.

drive-ins, girls wore bobby socks, and the guys drove Chevy Bel-Airs. It's made with crushed ice, chocolate *and* vanilla syrup, and milk. You must try one. In addition to unique ambiance, Angels boasts the distinction of being the oldest diner in Florida.

If you have time, pause in Palatka to take the walking/riding tour of the town and its more than 20 wonderful outdoor murals. The **Reverend Billy Graham** is honored by being depicted on one of them. He was chosen because he attended nearby **Florida Bible Institute,** was baptized in Putman county in 1938, and ordained as a minister of the gospels here in 1939.

As you leave Palatka on Routes 17/100 headed east, you'll cross the expansive St. Johns River into East Palatka. If Angels wasn't to your taste and you enjoy a more modern fast food chain, there is a Burger King in East Palatka that has a nice deck around back where you can eat overlooking the river. This is one spot only the locals know about and in the early spring with the gentle breeze from the water and a sack full of fries, you'll think you've died and gone to motorcycle heaven. There is also **Musselwhites's Seafood/Grill** (125 South Hwy 17, 386-326-9111) which serves better than average ribeye and shrimp.

From there you'll head south to Rt. 100 where you'll turn left toward **Bunnell.** This journey ends when you arrive at US 1 (Mile 146) in Bunnell, as it's a short hop south on US 1 back to Ormond and Bike Week madness.

Trip 7 Daytona's Famous "Loop"

Distance *22 miles*

It's a given that only a small portion of the several hundred thousand motor-cycle visitors who visit **Daytona** each year ever leave the confines of the party areas to actually explore the countryside and put some miles on their rides. Yet a large portion of the party crowd usually decides to take a break from walking endless vendor villages and the shoulder-to-shoulder madness that is Main Street, to ride what is known simply as "The Loop." Ordinarily a travel guide such as this one wouldn't list a 22 mile ride; it's much too short. However I know many of you will attend either **Bike Week** or **Biketoberfest** in Daytona and may only want a short break from the routines described above. The Loop is a perfect two hour diversion. Winding through **Tomoka Springs State Park,** the area is almost undeveloped residentially and commercially. Aside from the heavy motorcycle traffic you'll endure during the motorcycle rally weeks, there are almost no negatives to this ride. One caveat is the speed limit. Obey it without question. Traffic enforcement is steady and strict. Few, if any, warnings are given to speeders.

Daytona's famous loop winds through Tomoka State Park, on either side of the Halifax River. A word to the wise, obey the posted speed limit as the radar rangers don't have a sense of humor or a forgiving nature when it comes to speeding!

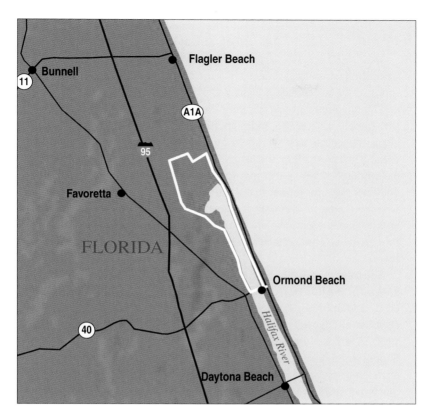

Start your loop ride on the west side of the **Halifax River** in **Ormond Beach** on North Beach Street at West Granada Boulevard. At 3.3 miles, you'll leave the residential world behind and enter Tomoka Springs State Park. Continue north as North Beach Street becomes Old Dixie Highway.

You'll feel as if you stepped back in time as you wind through the dense stands of stunted twisted oak and palm trees. It's easy to imagine a prehistoric creature stalking its prey among the sago palms that pack the forest floor. The actual park isn't very large and a few miles later you'll leave the official boundaries, but even then the scenery doesn't change much. You will notice, however, that civilization is beginning to encroach on this primitive area of Florida as developers build high dollar homes in the unprotected areas. In the not so distant future, this ride will no longer be recommended because of the residential congestion that is sure to accompany the pending development.

At 10.3 miles you'll turn right on Walter Boardman Road for 1.75 miles. At 11.5 miles you'll turn right again onto High Bridge Road. On your right will be **Bulow Creek** and most sunny days you'll pass someone trying to coax a fish

Bike Week at Daytona

Since the first motorcycle riders started coming to Daytona in the early spring, a lot has changed. Initially, the beach races were the attraction, and there were scant few other locations vying for the motorcycle tourists. Motels were cheap and plentiful. In the 80s, $49 per night rates along the beach were common and slightly cheaper rooms could be found a few blocks from the beach. Today, the supply has outstripped the demand and hoteliers use that reason to charge motorcyclists $200 to $400 per night for rooms, many with a five-night minimum stay. Nearby Orlando (home to Disneyland) has seen an influx of visiting bikers seeking a cheaper alternative and is now hosting motorcycle events during the same week as Daytona's event, and on average, lodging is cheaper there.

The Daytona party hot spots are Main Street (pick your favorite bar or hangout), The Iron Horse Saloon and Broken Spoke Saloon in Ormand on US 1, and Spotnik's Cabbage Patch on Tomoka Farms Road. South of Daytona in Edgewater is the Last Resort Bar. When it was built in the 1980s, The Last Resort was the last watering hole on US 1. Today it is infamous as the final hangout of serial killer Aileen Wuornos, who was arrested there on January 9, 1991. Wuornos was a highway prostitute who murdered seven middle-aged men and her life story was played by Charlize Theron in the movie *Monster*. 2nd Avenue is home to what is now referred to as Black Bike Week. After feeling shut out of the Main Street party in the early 50s, the locals organized a gathering that today has grown so large it almost rivals the crowd on Main Street.

Besides the party, there are vendors on almost every corner of town. The largest complex is Destination Daytona I-95 and US 1. This huge complex features the Harley-Davidson dealership as well as a hotel, condos, shops, restaurants, catalog stores, and vendors. US 1 south at Millers and Sunrise Mall Parking lot also has various manufacturers and vendors. The Speedway hosts demo rides, motorcycle manufacturers, custom builders, and vendors of every stripe. ■

HOTEL ORMOND

Hotel Ormond, named for Volusia County
pioneer James Ormond, was built in 1887 by
John Anderson and Joseph Price. The large
frame building was bought and enlarged by
Henry M. Flagler in the 1890's. Operated by
Flagler's Florida East Coast Railway, it was
one of the first Flagler hotels in Florida.
After 1890, the hotel and adjoining Ormond
Beach Golf Club became major Florida tourist
centers. John D. Rockefeller, a nearby resident,
was a patron of both.

Ormand is known as The Birthplace of Speed because the first auto races were staged here. Later they moved down the beach to Daytona. It is said that Henry Ford would come to those early races and sleep on the beach because he couldn't afford a room in the hotel. That was before he invented the Model A and the assembly line.

onto a line. At 13.3 miles you'll turn right again onto John Anderson Drive. The Loop ends at East Granada Boulevard. If you want to indulge in a bit of history, turn right and stop in at the circular building which is the visitor's station for the riverside park situated at the foot of the bridge. This building was once the turret on the **Ormond Hotel** built in 1887 and named for pioneer **James Ormond**. Railroad magnate **Henry M. Flagler** bought the building in the 1890s and it was operated by the **Flagler East Coast Railroad**. While Flagler went on to construct many other hotels in the Sunshine State, this was one of his first properties. Flagler's railroad was the first to connect the Keys with the rest of the United States. On September 2, 1935, over 500 people were killed when a massive Category 5 hurricane with an 18 foot tidal surge struck a full train of residents trying to escape to the mainland. The Key West railway was never rebuilt.

Ormond is also where the first auto races on the beach were held. Many people mistakenly think that it was Daytona Beach. **Henry Ford** himself once came to Ormond and slept on the beach because he couldn't afford a room in the hotel. Of course, his fortunes ultimately changed and he returned several years later with enough cash for a suite. In addition to automobiles, the Ormond Hotel was a magnet for golf lovers. Its register lists golfing greats such as **Slammin' Sam Snead, Gene Sarasen,** and **Babe Zaharias** among its guests. In 1923, **Ed Sullivan** (yes, that Ed Sullivan) was the Golf Secretary!

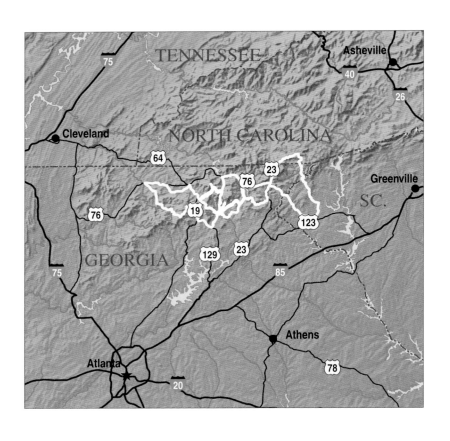

North Georgia Mountains

Three Rides to Erase Your Chicken Strip

A few years back a large boulder came crashing down and blocked one end of the access under Bridal Veils Falls. Geologists say the remaining rock is unstable so it's not recommended you try to duplicate this photograph.

The American South is blessed with some of the best motorcycle roads in the country. Although we didn't include North Carolina in this book, every motorcyclist worth his or her clutch knows about that famous road called **The Dragon** located in Western North Carolina near the area known as **Deals Gap**. If you're interested, check out *Motorcycle Journeys Through the Appalachians* by Dale Coyner from Whitehorse Press which includes the Dragon in its chapters. For this book I chose another great but lesser known motorcycle road, SR 180, **Wolf Pen Gap Road**. The "The Viper," as I like to call it, is a wickedly twisty stretch of blacktop that hasn't been as widely publicized as the Dragon, so it's not as heavily traveled as it has little or no commercial traffic. You will find farmers and locals who use the road frequently but since the only thing on SR 180 is the tiny town of **Suches**, home to **TWO, Two Wheels Only** motorcycle resort, there isn't much excuse or reason for tractor trailer drivers to use this route, as it doesn't save them any time.

In addition to TWO, **Copperhead Lodge** (www.copperheadlodge.com, 404-683-6654) is located in nearby Blairsville. Built by motorcycle enthusiasts for motorcycle enthusiasts, this resort features concerts and events during the riding season as well as short and long term rentals. Call ahead for pricing and availability.

For the three rides in this section we use **Helen** (www.helenga.org), as our hub. Located just a few quick hours north of Atlanta, Helen is an unabashed tourist town, although at certain times of the year it can be quiet and almost deserted. If you're the type of rider who is comfortable using electric gear and will ride year-round, then visit Helen after the **Oktoberfest** crowds have disappeared, usually around Thanksgiving and before Christmas. Now before you have me committed to an institution for suggesting you ride the mountains in the winter, understand that it snows infrequently in North Georgia and when it does, it's usually gone in a couple of days, as the temperatures rarely stay below freezing for any extended length of time. Having said that, there are spots along these rides where ice can and does accumulate in the shadows of the mountainside, so it's wise to always ride as if there is black ice around the next curve, because you never know. For accommodations I usually stay at the **Best Western** in Helen. The rates are reasonable, the rooms are clean, and they have wireless for my laptop that I'm forced to lug along. For the most part, Helen is a motorcycle friendly town; however, the biggest complaint I hear is the lack of parking. Admittedly, this is a problem and the poliz'e are inflexible when it comes to parking in loading zones or on yellow curbs. Yet the town isn't very large and you can easily walk to most of the shops from the hotels. Our favorite biker-friendly bar in Helen is the **Southside Bar and Grill** (7934 South Main Street, 706-878-2291). If you find yourself in need of leathers or boots, visit

Chattahoochee Biker Gear and **Das It Leathers** located at 8610 Helen High-way (706-878-0076). You'll find the prices reasonable and the owners helpful.

Using North Georgia as our base for the Three State Lasso run allows us to ride into the southern edge of North Carolina to the town of **Highlands** (www.highlandsinfo.com). There's something about this mountain town that just feels different. Of course it might have to do with the higher elevation where the air smells clean and fresher.

If waterfalls are your thing, I've outlined a side trip from Highland to **Bridal Veil Falls,** on scenic US 64, just 2.8 miles north of town. The falls originate 120 feet above and cascade over a rock outcropping. A few years ago, traffic was allowed to ride beneath the falls, but today a large boulder has fallen and blocked the path. I still highly recommend this detour; you won't be disappointed!

If you're in the mood for food while in Highlands, check out **Don Leon's Cafe** (30 Dillard Road, 828-526-1600, lunch Tuesday through Sunday 11 to 3 p.m., dinner Thursday through Saturday 5 to 8:30 p.m.) Rib lovers should try the **Rib Shack** (461 Spring Street, 828-526-2626) and burger lovers will want to sample **Hill Top Grill** (4th and Spring Street 828-526-5916, open for lunch Monday through Saturday).

Speaking of high elevation, the Brasstown Bald ride is a trip to Georgia's highest point, and one I always enjoy. If you love twisty roads, the ride up to the parking lot is peg-scraping heaven! I've been to Brasstown in every season and each season has its pluses and minuses. In the summer you get to see the flowers and smell the greenery but haze often obscures the surrounding mountains. There are also flowers in the spring, but a threat of showers can bring thunder and lightning, and since you're standing on the highest thing in the state, you become a living lightning rod. In the fall the tourists clog the highways but the views are wonderful so you put up with them. The winter season is the least desirable to visit but the cold crisp air does afford the hearty traveler with the farthest reaching views. At any time of year, you'll find the temperature 10 to 20 degrees colder on top than at the base. One winter I rode up, just because I'd never been in the winter and wanted to see what it was like. Since I was wearing heated gear the ride up was pleasant. However when I reached the parking lot and turned off the bike, the cold wind started cutting into my gear like a razor through paper and it wasn't long before I was ready to get back on the bike to warm up! Now telling someone that you had to get back on your bike to warm up in the winter isn't something you hear very often but I can attest to it.

Trip 8 Brasstown Bald Run

Distance *81 miles*
Terrain *Twisting, two-lane mountain roads, off-camber turns, wide, sweeping four-lane curves, and tight mountain ascent and descent. Traffic is light to moderate depending on the season and day of the week. To avoid the motorcycle crowds, mid-week is best.*
Highlights *Highest point in Georgia, waterfall. Wear good walking boots or take along a pair of tennis shoes for today's ride.*

Located in the **Blue Ridge Mountains, Helen** is rated the third largest tourist attraction in Georgia, behind Atlanta and Savannah. However, for the motorcycle tourists, I'd rank it #1 in Georgia since the mountain roads in this area are a motorcyclist's delight.

We'll start out today on Main Street or State Hwy 17. This route runs north and south through Helen and is just about the only way in or out of town. Reset your odometer when the road crosses over the **Chattahoochee River.** Country music fans will remember the song written by Alan Jackson, *Way Down Yonder on the Chattahoochee,* that celebrates this waterway. During the summer months, several companies rent inflated doughnut-shaped vinyl

Fed by underground springs and runoff, these two creeks converge to form Smith Creek which flows into the Chattahoochee and supplies much of Atlanta with drinking water.

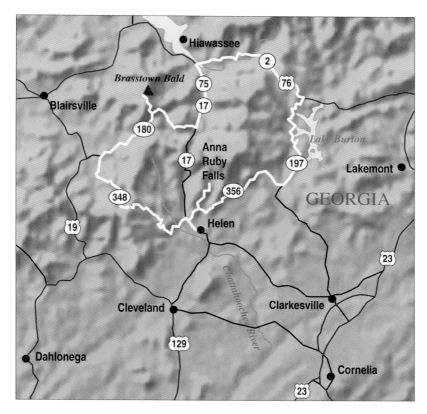

flotation devices (or *inner tubes,* as us country folks say) to vacationers to "Tube The Hootch." Even in August, the water stays cool and refreshing. The river's name comes from the Cherokee Native American language and it means *place of marked or flowered rocks.* Bring a pair of rubber water sandals since the river bottom is full of those marked rocks. There are also parts of the river that will be wide and shallow during summer droughts; you might have to walk a couple hundred feet towing your tube.

Head north out of town on SR 17. At Mile 1.1, turn right onto SR 356. In about 700 feet you'll see **Fred's Famous Peanuts** on the left (17 Clayton Road, Helen, 706-878-3124). You should take note of this location and return to it when you've finished riding for the day. Fred and Dianne Jenkins are the owners of this eclectic roadside stand which is open from spring to autumn. Their specialty? No, it's not hard boiled eggs…it's peanuts. Boiled, roasted, or fried. Oh, and Fred's has the only racquetball court for miles around, but that's probably not something you're interested in at this point, unless you happen to be a racquetball hustler and you're looking to get a game on.

Don't judge the food too harshly by the appearance from the parking lot. Joni's is one of those hidden jewels in North Georgia that the locals like to keep to themselves.

As you continue on SR 356, you'll come to Anna Ruby Falls Road on your left at Mile 2.4. Here again, take note; we're going to save this attraction until the end of the ride.

At Mile 12, turn left onto SR 197. I like this road so much that I recommend it several times during the rides that follow. You'll see why in the next five miles. The delightful twists and camber slopes create a ride challenging enough that even the serious sport bike crowd will enjoy it.

At Mile 17.1, you'll pass Laurel Lodge Road. If you're hungry, **Joni's Fireside Inn at Laurel Lodge** is just a mile down this road (115 Sweetwater Circle, Clarkesville, 706-947-1631). Hours vary depending on the season so call ahead. It isn't much to look at, but trust me on this one, Joni's is one of those local secrets that you will want to try. If you do, add two miles to these directions for the additional mileage.

At Mile 23.4, turn left onto US 76/SR 2. If a multiple lane road can be considered fun to ride, this one ranks at the top of motorcycle friendly four-lane highways in the state of Georgia. Enjoy the views as you cross **Muley Mountain** riding through the **Chattahoochee National Forest.**

At Mile 37, you'll turn left onto SR 75/17 and head south, and at Mile 42.8, you'll turn right on SR 180. In five miles, turn right again on 180 Spur and head toward **Brasstown Bald**, or **Mt. Enotah.** The Native Americans called this mountain Itseyi, which means "a place of fresh green," referring to its grassy knoll. Early white settlers mistook the Indian name for a similar one meaning brass. So that's how the mountain came to be known as Brasstown Bald. According to Cherokee legend, there was once a great flood and all men died except for a few Cherokee families who landed on top of Brasstown Bald in a giant canoe. The Great Spirit killed all the trees on top of the mountain so the survivors could plant crops and live until the floods subsided. This three mile section up to the mountain top is steep, twisty, and will have you wondering if your brakes are up to the task on the return downhill ride. Soon you'll enter the parking lot ($2 fee). Here's where your feet will thank me for suggesting comfortable shoes. If you didn't heed my advice, then I suggest you pay the additional fee to ride the shuttle bus to the observation deck at the top. Be advised that if you decide to walk, the half-mile paved path is steep, but there are benches to catch your breath. You'll think you're *bad* out of shape, but blame it on the thinner air, not the extra biscuit at breakfast. On clear days, the 360-degree view from the observation tower atop the mountain allows you to see four states, Georgia, Tennessee, North Carolina, and South Carolina. You might even see Big Foot!

THE ROUTE FROM HELEN

0   Start in downtown Helen, Georgia, Hwy 17 at Chattahoochee River Bridge
1.1   Turn right on SR 356
12.0   Turn left on SR 197
17.0   Turn right on Laurel Lodge Road
18.0   Return to turn right on SR 197
24.5   Turn left on US 76/SR 2
37.5   Turn left on 75/17 (Unicoi Turnpike)
43.9   Turn right on SR 180
49.2   Turn right on 180 Spur toward Brasstown Bald
52.3   Arrive in Brasstown Bald
55.4   Turn right on SR 180
61.7   Turn left on SR 348 (Richard B. Russell Scenic Highway)
74.1   Turn left on SR 75
76.8   Turn left SR 356
78.1   Turn left on Anna Ruby Falls Road
81.5   Arrive in Anna Ruby Falls

After you've taken in the view, backtrack down 180 Spur to Hwy 180 and turn right. At Mile 60.7, turn left onto **Richard B. Russell Scenic Highway.** Opened in 1965, This 14 mile route takes you across the **Appalachian Trail** and affords spectacular views of the Blue Ridge Mountains. It will be clogged with traffic from late September to early November as the overlooks showcase the beauty of the changing colors on the hardwood trees below. I enjoy this area in the dead of winter because there's little traffic then, but be warned, once the winter arrives, ice buildup on the area roads can be hazardous, even on mild temperature days. I remember riding once in December to the crest of this highway. On one side of the mountain, the road was clear, but as soon as I entered the opposite side into an area that stays in the shadow of the mountain almost all day, the ice was everywhere except the very center of the two-lane road! Fortunately I wasn't traveling very fast and was able to negotiate the 200 yard stretch without difficulty, but had I been knee dragging, the results wouldn't have been pleasant.

The footpath to Georgia's highest point atop Brasstown Bald is steep and can be a challenge for veterans of the buffet wars, like myself. For a fee you can catch a shuttle bus ride to the top, my preferred choice.

A few hundred yards from this photo the Richard B. Russell Parkway winds around the other side of the mountain which doesn't get a lot of sun, and the ice was covering all but one lane. It was too hazardous to stop for a photograph!

At Mile 73.1, turn left on SR 75, and at Mile 75.5, turn right to stay on SR 75/17. In just .3 miles turn left again on SR 356 for our trip to **Anna Ruby Falls** (www.fs.fed.us/conf, 706-754-6221) on Anna Ruby Falls Road. There is a $2 per vehicle fee to enter the park, which is just 3 miles down the road. If you had your fill of climbing at Brasstown Bald you'll be tempted to skip this part of the journey; but if you do, you'll miss one of the showcases of the North Georgia Mountains. This half-mile trek to the base of the twin falls is slightly less strenuous than the hike up Brasstown Bald and I planned it that way. If you made that hike, this one's a cake-walk. Anna Ruby Falls marks the junction of Curtis and York Creeks that combine to form Smith Creek. Curtis Creek drops the farthest at 153 feet and York drops 50 feet. Smith Creek empties into Unicoi Lake and then into the Chattahoochee eventually emptying into the Gulf of Mexico 550 miles later. After the Civil War, **Colonel John H. "Captain" Nichols** purchased the surrounding land and quite accidentally discovered the falls one day while on horseback. Colonel Nichols adored his only daughter, Anna Ruby, as she was all he had left after the death of his two infant sons and his wife. He named the twin waterfalls "Anna Ruby" in his daughter's honor. It's hard to imagine, but logging operations at the turn of the century completely stripped the hardwoods from Captain Nichols' land surrounding the falls. When you return, you can backtrack to SR 356. Don't forget Fred's on your right before you reach SR 75/17, and turn left to return to Helen.

Trip 9   Riding the Viper

Distance *117 miles*

Terrain *Wide, sweeping curves on well-maintained asphalt highway, tight, tortured, hairpin curves on the Viper with several elevation changes. Long two-lane roads through rural north Georgia. Traffic is light to moderate depending on the season and day of the week. To avoid the motorcycle crowds, mid-week is best.*

Highlights *Georgia's highest lake, Wolf Pen Gap, Two Wheels Only motorcycle resort, 1928 vintage restaurant, twisty four lane highways that were made for motorcycle journeys!*

Start your trip in downtown **Helen** where Hwy 17 crosses the river and head north out of town. At Mile 1.4, turn left on SR 75 and ride to Mile 9.5 and turn right on US 129/SR 11.

Pappy's Trading Post is a favorite pit stop of mine when traveling this north Georgia route. Just be careful in the gravel parking lot.

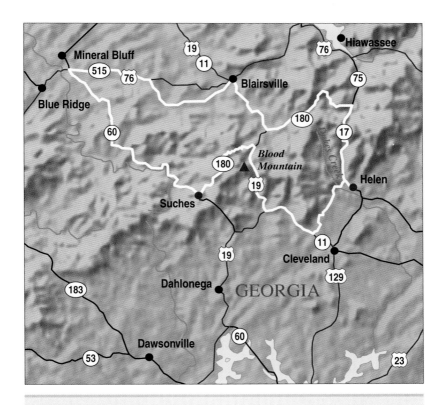

THE ROUTE FROM HELEN

0   Start in downtown Helen, Georgia, Hwy 17 at Chattahoochee
         River Bridge

1.4   Turn left on SR 75

9.5   Turn right on US 129/SR 11

16.5   Go straight on SR 11/129

27.1   Turn left on SR 180 (Wolf Pen Gap Road)

38.1   Turn right on SR 60

65.6   Turn right on US 76/515/2

86.5   Turn right on US 129 SR 11 (Cleveland Street)

92.0   Stop at Pappy's Trading Post

94.5   Turn left on SR 180

107.0 Turn right on SR 17/SR 75

118.0 Arrive in downtown Helen

In the winter, Pappy's Trading Post has an open fireplace and hot cider mull really hits the spot!

At 16.5 miles, you'll pass **Turner's Corner Cafe**, a 1928 vintage restaurant and popular motorcycle gathering place. Once operated as a gas station and rural country store, Turner's no longer pumps gas or sells grocery items. It's still a favorite meeting place for the local motorcyclists, however, and the food is quite good. You can sit inside, or outside on the balcony overlooking the **Chestatee River.** Try any of the homemade pies (pronounced paaahz) for dessert. As you leave Turner's Corner continue north on 19/129 up **Blood Mountain.** Local folklore has it that the mountain got its name long before white men came to the area. After a great battle between the Cherokee and the Creek Nations, so many braves were killed that their blood ran down the mountain turning it red. This seems to be a true tale as Indian names were also given to nearby Slaughter Creek and Slaughter Gap. To the Cherokee, Blood Mountain was sacred because it was the home of the Nunnehi, the spirit people who watched over hunters and hikers in the area.

On my last trip in this area, the Nunnehi must have been watching over me because I was enjoying a spirited ride up SR 129 in the mid-morning hours. The traffic was light and I had become one with my motorcycle, leaning into the curves, and using both northbound lanes to carve this road as I never had before. I was feeling quite good about the trip when something unusual caught my eye and I immediately slowed down and tried to see what it was in my rear view mirror. As I rounded the next curve at about half speed, I rode headlong into a patch of sand covered with diesel fuel! I knew it was diesel by the smell. I almost couldn't believe my dumb luck because there was no reason to suspect any hazard on this highway and I've never seen anything like it before or since. As it turned out, there were three similar patches on this road a mile or so apart. I never discovered the true source of my initial distraction, but there's no doubt that I would've gone down on that first patch had I not slowed to see what it was.

At Mile 27.1, you'll turn left onto SR 180 also known as Wolf Pen Gap Road. I remember "discovering" Wolf Pen Gap Road quite by accident a few years ago. I was scouting a route for a poker run, came upon this road, and decided to see where it would lead me. When I arrived at SR 60 almost 12 miles later I'm sure I shouted something like "YES!" I'd ridden Deals Gap (The Dragon) in North Carolina, and immediately decided that my new find was worthy of being named "The Viper." There are two man-made lakes, constructed by the **CCC (Civilian Conservation Corp)** on this stretch of premium motorcycle blacktop. At Mile 27.5 is the entrance to **Vogel State Park and Lake Trahlyta** (www.ngeorgia.com/parks/vogel.html). This 20-acre lake

For advertising to be successful it must first attract the attention of the public. This advertisement for boiled peanuts is a textbook case. If you didn't know that the name of this establishment is Poor Boyz, you might be left wondering what being poor had to do with anything.

was named for the Cherokee maiden that is buried at Stonepile Gap at the intersection of US 19 and SR 60. At Mile 33.7, you'll pass the entrance to **Lake Winfield Scott** (www. georgiatrails.com/places/winfieldscott.html), the highest lake in Georgia.

At Mile 38, CR 180 deadends at SR 60 in the town of **Suches.** Just south of this intersection is the well-known motorcycle destination, **TWO (Two Wheels Only) motorcycle resort** (3580 State Hwy 60, 706-747-5151). Operated by GT and Britt Turner, TWO offers camping, a four-bedroom lodge, and a fully furnished two-bedroom mobile home. They also boast of having the only Wi-Fi internet connection for miles around. Closed during the winter months, TWO usually opens around the end of March for the season. If you're coming to TWO, heed their firm policy that all guests must either be riding a motorcycle or towing one. If you're hungry, ask about the Big Ass Sirloin Burger. Lunch is available on Saturday and Sunday 11 to 2 p.m., Dinner on Friday and Saturday 5:30 to 8:30 p.m. Check the resort's website (www.twowheelsonly.com) for a listing of weekend events. If you're there in the fall, try to time your visit to the 50 cc rally in October, called the True Grits Fun Run. This event, started in 1982, raises money for the local volunteer fire

TWO, Two Wheels Only, is a popular motorcycle destination in North Georgia with overnight accommodations and lunch served daily during the riding season.

department. Watching or joining grown men and women speeding (well almost speeding) for 60 miles around the North Georgia mountains is worth the trip. Browse their website for photos from past rallies and you'll see what I mean.

When you leave TWO, head north on SR 60 toward the town of **Mineral Bluff.** Stay on 60 through a couple of turns until you reach US 76/SR 2/515 and turn right.

At Mile 87, you'll turn right onto US 129/SR 11, and at Mile 92, you'll pass **Pappy's Trading Post,** an eclectic blend of different businesses with that certain feel of roadside kitsch. The parking lot is gravel and sometimes soft gravel as the proprietor of Pappy's Trading Post informed me one fine day. "The EPA won't let us pave the lot because of the river that runs directly behind the lot, so all we can do is keep putting gravel in every year. I estimate we have about 20 feet of compacted gravel by now beneath your motorcycle, but every year the clay rises to the top and we have to add more gravel." If you're uncomfortable on gravel you can park at the south entrance on the few feet of asphalt there and walk to the different stores. At one time, Pappy, a retired firefighter from Florida, built and owned all the buildings at the Trading Post, but as he approached the time for his second retirement, he began to sell off individual parts of the complex. Now almost each business is individually owned. There's a restaurant on site but I haven't tried it so I can't say much about it. In the winter, the Trading Post keeps a fire burning in the outside fireplace and the homemade cider mull is welcome, warm refreshment while you sit on the back porch and watch the **Nottely River** flowing by.

Return to US 129 and head south to Mile 94.5 where you'll turn left on SR 180. At Mile 107 turn right on 75/17 and enjoy the last few miles of this journey on the twisty section of the Unicoi Turnpike. It's a nice ending to a ride you won't soon forget.

Trip 10   Three State Lasso Run

Distance   *158 miles*

Terrain   *Two lane except short stretch on US 441. A few tight, twisting turns with elevation changes in a few places. Traffic is light to moderate in the country, heavy in town.*

Highlights   *Twisty two lane roads, mountain towns, lakeside views, covered bridge, working grist mill, winery, family style lunch, abandoned railroad tunnel*

The sign reads "Gas 9.3 cents per gallon. Tax 4.5 cents per gallon. Total price 13.8 cents per gallon," and back then you had someone willing to pump it for you!

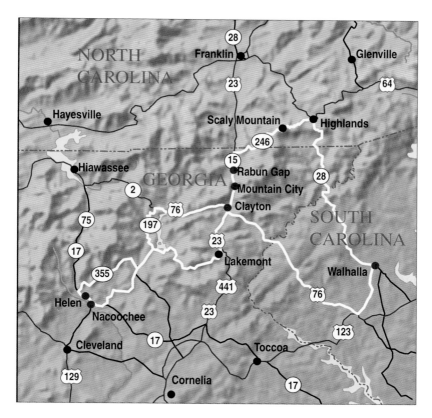

We start our three state journey in downtown **Helen**, Georgia. I chose Helen for our base in the North Georgia mountains because of its central location and like it or not, because it's a tourist town with services and restaurants within walking distances of the hotels. For lodging, the **Best Western** is my choice for the best value. Avoid the **Helendorf River Inn**, as I found it to be not motorcycle friendly. There are a host of other lodging opportunities and cabins, most of which are motorcycle friendly. Often after a long day in the saddle, I like to take a hot bath and unwind before eating and sometimes it's inconvenient to get all the gear back on for a short one or two mile jaunt to eat. Helen has enough restaurants that I can skip the gear and walk downtown to **Paul's Steakhouse,** or for German food, there's **Hans**. If Mexican is to your taste, there's a good one in the rear of what used to be the outlet mall, next to the city park. Speaking of the city park, I guess this is as good a time as any to plug the *USRiderNews* Reunion Run. For the past six years we've hosted a motorcycle rally in this town on the first full weekend in June. It's a laid back event with just enough people and vendors so you don't feel overwhelmed with

Covered bridges like this are disappearing from our southern landscape and one day will exist only in photographs. Visit them while you can.

the crowds. Only advertised in *USRiderNews,* it's attended by a few thousand readers—just a few old friends getting together, swapping stories, and riding some good mountain roads. For more information you can check out the website, www.usridernews.com/reunion.

As you head south out of town on SR 17, you'll enter the village of **Nacoochee.** You won't notice any increase in traffic because the whole village consists of a couple of stores and a working grist mill. Actually there are no houses or permanent residents to speak of but it does have its own web site (www.nacoocheevillage.com). Since you just got started, you might want to save a stop here until you return to Helen at the end of this ride. Whichever you decide, be sure to take the time to stop in at **Nora Mill** (www.noramill.com) for a trip back in time to when corn grinding was essential to the survival of the early settlers. This water-powered mill was established in 1876 and thanks to Ron Fain and his family, is still in operation today. They grind corn daily using either the original French burr stones that are water powered by the **Chattahoochee River**—or by a more modern "Meal Master" stone grinding system located on the second floor. Both methods produce the products they sell such as stone ground grain, corn meal, pancake, muffin, and bread mix. This is an excellent opportunity for our visitors from north of the Mason-Dixon Line to uncover the secrets of the grits making process. Think of how smart you'll sound the next time one of your Yankee friends asks "What are grits?"

THE ROUTE FROM HELEN

0	Start in downtown Helen, Georgia, Hwy 17 at Chattahoochee River Bridge
1.7	Turn left to stay on SR 17
4.0	Turn left on SR 255
11.8	Stay straight on SR 197 N
15.7	Turn right on Burton Dam Road
18.6	Road changes to Seed Lake Road
23.0	Road changes to Lake Rabun Road
29.2	Turn left on Old Hwy 441
30.7	Turn right on Main Street to reach US 441/23
30.8	Turn left on US 441/23
43.4	Turn right on Henry Dillard Street
43.6	Turn right on Franklin Street to Dillard House Restaurant
44.5	Return to 441/23 via Franklin Street, keeping right to head north
45.2	Turn right onto SR 106/246
59.5	Turn right onto 64/28 (Main Street)
59.7	Turn right on South 4th Street to stay on SR 28
89.3	Turn right on SR 183 (South College Street)
96.8	Turn right on US 76—Long Creek Highway turns into Lookout Mountain Scenic Highway
123.5	Continue straight across 441/23 to pick up 76 west
124.0	Turn left on US 76/SR 2
134.0	Turn left on SR 197
142.3	Turn right on SR 356
156.6	Turn left on SR 75/17 to starting point in downtown Helen

The first question visitors from outside of the South ask is "where do grits come from?" The answer is Nora Mills. Actually not all southern grits are made here but this is an authentic working grist mill that still produces grits and cornmeal the old fashioned way.

Across the highway is the **Habersham Winery** (www.habersham-winery.com, 770-983-1973), a much newer addition to the village but still interesting. Established in 1983 and open daily for complimentary testing and an area where you can watch the wine making process. Don't get too happy with the samples, junior, as you're on two wheels and in my neck of the woods and I'm not too fond of wino bikers!

As you leave Nacoochee Village, turn left to continue on Rt. 17. You'll notice a covered gazebo on a fairly large mound of earth in the field to your right. This is known as the **Nacoochee Indian Mound.** 190 feet long, 150 feet wide, and 20 feet high, the mound stood in the center of the ancient Cherokee town of **Gauxule.** But, it predates even the Cherokees and was most probably built by the pre-historic Mississippian Culture known as "Mound Builders." Visited by de Soto in 1540 in his search for gold, the mound was the location of a ceremonial town house where the sacred fire burned unceasingly and sacred dances were held. The gazebo atop the mound was built in the 1800s by John H. Nichols, a wealthy landowner.

You'll continue on to Sautee where you'll turn left on SR 255 (Mile 4.2) and head north. At Mile 6.7, you'll pass **Stovall Covered Bridge** in a park on your right. At only 36.8 feet long, it's the smallest covered bridge in Georgia. While it's no longer in use, you can pull off and park your bike near it for a good photo opportunity. Add it to your "this is my bike beside a covered bridge photo collection" that all good motorcycle tourists seem to have.

My Grandma's Lace Cornbread

Before you attempt this recipe you must have a cast iron skillet which has been properly seasoned. A brand new skillet won't work near about as well. If you don't have one, see if you can borrow one. If that's not possible, then buy a new one, but never, ever wash an iron skillet in the dishwasher. When you're finished cooking with it, hand wash it, and before storing it, rub a thin layer of animal fat, i.e., Crisco or other lard all over to prevent rust and to keep it properly seasoned.

5 cups cornmeal

1 1/2 cups hot water, or more as needed

1 tsp. salt

Crisco or cooking oil as needed

Cast iron skillet (no exceptions)

Mix the meal, water, and salt together in a large mixing bowl into a thin consistency. The more water you use, the thinner your lace edges will be. This is where beginners make the most mistakes. It takes some experience to gauge the correct amount. Too much water and the mixture will not hold together, too little and you won't get the thin lace around the edge.

Pour enough oil into the skillet (or melt Crisco) to about 1/2 an inch in an 8-inch skillet. Heat the oil, but don't let it start to smoke. You can tell it's ready by letting a little water drip into the grease. It will sizzle and "fry." Use caution as this is where many a new bride has damaged her kitchen by becoming distracted and allowing the grease to catch up (catch fire). If that should happen, turn off the heat and smother the flames with a skillet cover, don't try to move it and don't throw water on it or you'll burn your house down!

When the oil is just right, pour about 1/4 cup of the cornmeal water mixture into the middle of the pan letting it spread out. The trick is to keep the middle thicker than the edges. As your cornbread cooks, the water evaporates from the edges first, giving it that lace appearance. Make sure the mixture floats in the oil, or it will stick to the pan and you won't be able to turn it after about 1 minute. Use a wide spatula, and take care not to splash hot grease on the stove. After another minute, your lace cornbread will be golden brown, about as thick as a coin in the middle, and crunchy around the lace edges. Remove it from your skillet, add oil as needed, and repeat the process, until all your mixture is used. ∎

At Mile 11.7, you'll come to the intersection of Hwy 197 and the **Old Batesville General Store and Restaurant** (11801 Hwy 197, North Clarkesville, 706-947-3434). Before the automobile shrank the size of the county, this white millboard, rusted tin roof building was the trading post for everyone living in the area. Over time it became obvious that the restaurant side of the business was much more profitable than the grocery side so it followed the inevitable evolution of many businesses of this size. The sign boasts that you will find the "Best Biscuits in Batesville" here, and after sampling their freshly made home cooked variety, I can't dispute their claim. Open for breakfast and lunch everyday and dinner Thursday through Saturday nights, it's best visited in October for the **Batesville Historic Celebration** (www.batesvilledays.com).

After you've enjoyed your fill of home cooking, continue north on Hwy 197 to Mile 15.7 where you'll turn right onto Burton Dam Road. Depending on the time of year you visit, this road will either be jam-packed or nearly deserted. It's a great winding road that runs alongside the **Talluah River** which flows through the **Nacoochee, Seed,** and **Rabun Lakes.** What's not so great is the amount of traffic when vacation season is in full swing. Take your time and watch for cars entering and leaving the driveways of the many homes along this section of the highway. In the wintertime, the lakes are all but deserted and the ride is more enjoyable, except for the temperature which averages in the low 30s. At various points along this route the road name will change from Burton Dam Road to Seed Lake Road to Joy King Lane to Lake Rabun Road. You won't notice the change unless you're looking at the road signs. At Mile 29.2, you'll turn left on old Hwy 441 and in just over one mile, you'll turn left to reach US 441. The last time I visited in 2005, GADOT was reconstructing the intersection here. If this access is still blocked, continue straight and take the first paved road back to your right. At whatever point, you'll need to turn left on 441 to continue north toward the town of Clayton.

There are many restaurants in Clayton and since we'll be looping through later on this journey we'll motor through it for now. Continue toward the towns of **Mountain City** and **Rabun Gap.** At Mile 43.3, you'll turn right on Henry Dillard Street. In .2 of a mile, turn right on Franklin Street to take a seat at this region's best known restaurant, **The Dillard House Inn and Restaurant** (www.thedillardhouse.com). Founded in 1917 by Carrie and Arthur Dillard, their six room boarding house became a favorite stopover for travelers primarily due to the culinary talents of Carrie Dillard. She was also as good a business woman as a cook and this once modest bed-and-breakfast has become a complex of 70 modern motel rooms and 25 cottages and chalets. Notable visitors have included **Henry Ford, Thomas Edison, Lady Bird Johnson, Walt Disney,** and former **President Jimmy Carter.** Open every day for breakfast, lunch and dinner, be sure to bring your appetite and your wallet. The food is served family style, which simply means instead of ordering a couple of items from a printed menu, your server will bring you a bowl or platter of everything on the menu for the day! If, for instance, you and your friends are fried chicken lovers and there isn't enough to go around, in true family style your server will bring you more. Dessert is included but your drinks are not. The upshot to all this food is a bill that's just as super-sized as the meal. Lunch will set you back about $20 per person. Lucky for me they accept all the major credit cards or the IRS wouldn't have believed that expense report! If you're in need of overnight accommodations, rates start at $69 and top out at $169 per night during the peak season for a Jacuzzi suite.

When leaving, take Franklin Street north to where it intersects with US 441 and turn right on 441. At Mile 45.2 turn right on SR 106/246, and about two miles later, you'll enter North Carolina. For the next fourteen miles you'll ride along the **Blue Ridge Divide** toward the town of Highlands, North Carolina. At Mile 59.1, turn right on US 64 to enter **Highlands.** The locals like to boast that if you drew an imaginary line from New Orleans to New York City and another from Chicago to Savannah the intersection of those two lines would be downtown Highlands. Of course, I'm not sure why we'd want to draw these imaginary lines, but it keeps simple minds like me occupied for hours on end! If you're hungry, try the **Highlands Pizza Place** (365 Main Street, 828-526-

The best biscuits in Batesville can be found here, at the Batesville General Store, which actually is no longer a store, but a restaurant!

5660). The Chicken Cesar Salad is good, as is the calzone, and of course, the pizza. You'll have to bus your own tables but there's a television in the back if you're jonesing for the football game or a race you might be missing. While you're downtown you might have a hankering to wander the interesting shops full of antiques and collectibles, or not. If pizza isn't really your thing, try the **Rib Shack** (460 Spring Street, lunch served 11 to 2 p.m., and dinner 5 to 8 p.m.).

While we're on the subject of food, I should probably warn my northern friends who might be visiting this area. If you're in the mood to argue, then there are four subjects that are sure-fire argument starters. The first is politics, the second is religion, the third is college football, and the fourth is barbeque. Now, the barbeque at the Rib Shack is different and it has its own unique flavor but don't tell your friends it's delicious because that will start an argument. Besides the pork and beef barbeque on the menu (beef is my personal favorite at this restaurant), there are black eyed peas which aren't really black eyed peas at all. What they serve here are purple hulled peas, which have a slight green color, a distinctive flavor, and are different from black eyed peas. Not that I'm in the mood to argue, you understand, but being from the deep South, it's important to know your legumes.

One restaurant in town that I've yet to try but comes highly recommended is **Don Leon's** (Hwy 106 and Main Street, 828-526-1600), serving lunch Tuesday through Sunday 11 to 3 p.m., and dinner Tuesday through Saturday 5 to 8 p.m.

Side Trip: Bridal Veil and Cullasaja Waterfalls

Since you're this close, you really should take a short detour to see **Bridal Veil Falls** just 2.5 miles from downtown Highlands. To get there take US 64 west, and as you round a curve the falls will be on your right, you can't miss them. Years ago, the road passed directly under the falls, and even after the highway department re-routed the highway around the falls, the pavement remained so you could ride under the spray. However, a large rock slide has blocked the path so you can no longer ride under the falls. If you're feeling adventurous you might ride under the spray and turn around but be careful as the highway stays wet and there isn't much room to maneuver. If you just have to get that photograph, I'd recommend backing your bike down under the falls. However, use caution because not that long ago, that big rock you see blocking your path came down without warning and if more of those let loose while you're posing for a photo, there isn't a helmet in the world that would save you from instant compaction! Bridal Veil isn't the only beautiful waterfall long US 64. There's also **Cullasaja**

Falls, which is about 6 miles farther west. Cullasaja Falls are the most spectacular waterfalls in North Carolina (in my opinion) and they're also the most dangerous to view. The parking area is only about 6 feet wide and will be on your left side as you approach. Since you're going to be returning to Highlands after viewing the falls, I recommend you travel past the pull off to an area farther along where you'll feel comfortable turning around to return to the falls, since there's no way you're going to be able to safely turn around and park along this narrow space.   ■

When you're ready, continue on SR 28 South 4th Street. In a few miles the local designation turns into Walhalla Road, because you're heading into the town of Walhalla.

At Mile 65.5, you'll cross into South Carolina, our third state in this three state lasso journey.

As you enter the town of **Walhalla,** you'll see on your left a **Confederate Memorial** that is common to many towns in the South. If it looks familiar, it's because it's on the cover of this book! At Mile 89.5, turn right on SR 183, South College Street. At Mile 97, turn right on US 76 (Long Creek Highway) and at Mile 104 you'll enter the **Sumter National Forest.** While the designation changes to the **Chattahoochee National Forest** after you cross the **Chatooga River** at Mile 114, the scenery remains pretty much the same along this route, which becomes Lookout Mountain Scenic Highway a few miles outside Clayton, Georgia.

At Mile 122.8, you'll return to US 441 in **Clayton,** Georgia. If you're hungry, there is the usual chain variety fare, but if you want something different and it's either a Friday or Saturday, try **Buck Creek Tavern** (88 North Main Street, 706-212-0101). Here is rustic decor with a tavern feel—and a great Jack Daniels Steak. **Granny's Kuntry Kitchen** (Hwy 441 South, 706-782-3914) is a bit more eclectic with home-style Mexican and Greek food, and is open six days a week, breakfast through dinner.

If you're not in the mood to stop, or once you've satisfied your needs, stay on US 76/2 west through Clayton, a fun stretch of asphalt without a lot of traffic. The designation **Lookout Mountain Scenic Highway** is a bit misleading as there are few scenic overlooks or mountaintop views to enchant you. Still, during the spring when the dogwoods are in bloom the highway is a joy to ride.

At Mile 134, turn left on SR 197 and for the next 11 miles you'll enjoy some of the best tight twisties on this route. At Mile 155, turn right on SR 356 to return to SR 17 and then at Mile 156, turn left to return to Alpine Helen. Remember if you skipped the Nacoochee village, now's the time to return for the grits making tour at the grist mill and a taste of the winery.

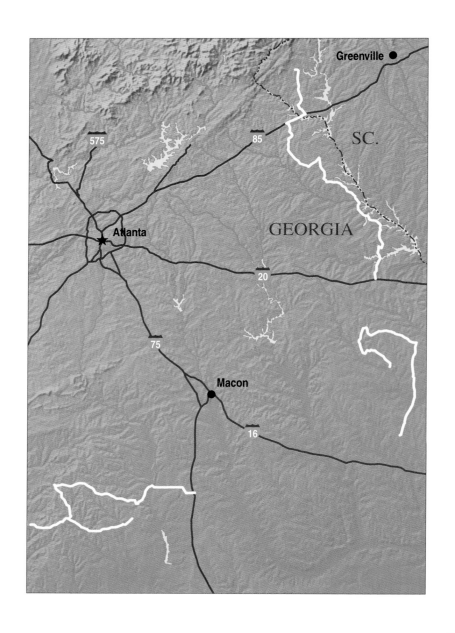

Fish Camps, Guidestones, & Canyons

The Georgia You Might Not Know

There was a time when I was sure I knew where to find all the interesting places in Georgia. Then I discovered **Georgia's Little Grand Canyon** and **Westville,** a working 1800s village and suddenly I knew I didn't know all that I thought I knew. I'd lived here for 40 years and traversed this state more times than a gubernatorial candidate but, this was proof that I'd missed at least two quite interesting destinations.

So that started me thinking about what else I may have missed, and I'm proud to say that I'm still finding little out-of-the-way spots to visit. Finding previously unknown travel treasures this close to home is just about as good as it gets, plus it provides me with endlessly odd trivia to spout off at bike nights.

Bald Cypress was once very important to the economy of the South because it's resistant to rot and decay, easy to work with simple tools, and makes beautiful cabinets and furniture. High demand in the early 1900s almost completely destroyed accessible southern swamp forests.

Folks come from miles around just to eat at Yoder's Deitsch Haus near Montezuma, Georgia. In case the name didn't give it away, Yoder's is a Mennonite owned restaurant and bakery which is a must-stop destination if you're the least bit hungry!

Speaking of odd, I remember the first time I "discovered" **Elberton's Guidestones.** Actually it occurred on a ride to Winder with Randy Clark, a good friend of mine. I wanted to feature a company there in my newly formed motorcycle magazine, *Dixie Rider.* Sitting out in the middle of nowhere on a lonely stretch of two lane black top was this smaller version of England's Stonehenge. I remember thinking how odd this place was and wondering at its purpose. Isn't that like human beings to feel the need to put everything in its place? Everything has to have a purpose, and a reason for being where and what it is. The mystique of the purpose is what brings people to places like this. Okay, I'm getting all meta-physical now and starting to chant mantras in my head.

Getting back to reality, another little gem I discovered was in **Royston,** Georgia, and was the quite unassuming museum of baseball legend **Ty Cobb** (www.tycobbmuseum.org). When I first pulled up I thought I'd made a wrong turn and ended up in a medical office complex. Then, I realized that Cobb's museum is in fact located inside the Joe A. Adams Professional Building across the way from the county hospital. If you love baseball history, you'll want to make this a "don't miss attraction" on this trip. While he had a reputation as a rough and rowdy player, Cobb was a shrewd businessman and used his talents on the field to build his wealth off the field. Remember this was before the era of multi-million dollar contracts and big signing bonuses. Cobb commercially endorsed another local brand, Coca-Cola in it's infancy, and was one of the very few players in his time to receive the type of corporate advertising deals so common today. Yet, Cobb was a generous man who donated much of his wealth to ensure that his fellow rural Georgians of both races could receive quality medical care.

Then there is Providence Canyon, also known as Georgia's Little Grand Canyon in the southwest corner of the state. The photos I took don't really do justice to what is essentially unchecked erosion on a major scale. The largest portion of the canyon was created in the 1800s because of poor farming practices which allowed the topsoil to wash away. Today the headwaters of **Turner Creek** rise up from the floor of the canyon and once combined with the continual south Georgia rain will cause the canyon to grow deeper and wider over the next few centuries. Tell your grandkids to tell their grandkids to tell their grandkids that you visited it before it became famous. As for famous, there is no doubt in my mind that if the state of Georgia brought a major highway, such as an Interstate, near the town of **Lumpkin,** the tourists would visit in droves. As it is, Lumpkin is really "off the beaten path." Despite having two hidden gems, Westville, a working 1800s village, and **Providence Canyon State Park,** it doesn't attract very many tourists. This makes it appealing to me because it's isolated and I'm not real fond of standing in line to see stuff.

We'll also visit **Montezuma,** a town rich in history and good food. I have my in-laws to thank for first introducing me and my ever expanding waistline to **Yoder's Deitsch Haus** just outside of Montezuma. If you're like me and eating ranks as high as riding the twisties, then Mennonite cooking will taste like carving a mountain road on a Yamaha R-1.

The only thing I like as much as eating and riding is visiting Civil War sites. Just south of Montezuma is **Andersonville,** one of the most maligned sites in that tragic period of our country's history. Besides the Civil War, you'll find the visitors center has a well constructed museum dedicated to POWs of all wars.

Aviation buffs will recall **Americus** as the place where **Charles Lindbergh** made his first solo flight. There is a monument to Lindbergh on the grounds of Souther Field and the last time I visited I arrived a half hour before sundown on Sunday to find the airport virtually deserted. As I stood reading the inscription on the monument dedicated to that milestone in U.S. history, a single engine plane flew low over my head. I glanced up half expecting to see the dual wings and wooden prop of a Curtis "Jenny" and the leather cap and goggles of the famous aviator himself sitting inside the open cockpit. You'll find that the heavy hand of progress hasn't spoiled the area. The mystique of the man whose

If you're not careful you'll take some of the red clay from Georgia's Little Grand Canyon home with you. It's amazing how sticky it becomes when it gets around your riding boots!

life's journey began in Americus at Souther Field and culminated in Paris at Le Bourget Field can still be felt in the quiet rustle of the wind through the Georgia pines.

While we're on the subject of the unspoiled, **Plains** is a town that time seems to have passed by. It's interesting to note that not much has changed since that day in December, 1974, when **James Earl Carter,** a little-known Democratic candidate from Georgia stood on the railroad depot and announced to the world that he would become the 39th President of the U.S. Carter went on to fulfill that prediction and today the entire town is a living history exhibit. You won't find any strip malls or super Wal-Marts here, just old fashioned values and simple south Georgia country folk who work their farms day in and day out, the same way they've done for generations.

I was tempted to break this ride up into two days because Andersonville, Westville, and Plains are sites that require more than a cursory visit, at least for the history buff. In the end I decided that not everyone loves to immerse themselves in the past as much as I do. But, quite honestly I cannot do this ride in one day. So, if you're like me, allow an extra day, and using Americus as your hub, take your time to really explore the sites to truly see it all. You'll be glad you did.

How could I write my first book without including a trip through the towns of my youth? The problem was that the area of Georgia I grew up in is almost entirely devoid of twisty motorcycle roads, or at least the paved kind. I would have to find some other attraction or history fact to lure readers. But, the area isn't known for famous people or historical battles. Then one day it hit me like the tail of a big mouth bass, I would highlight a fish camp tour!

Since owning my first Harley-Davidson, my motto has been, "Ride to Eat, Eat to Ride," and what better way to introduce central Georgia than a tour of three of its well known fish camps. Both **McKinney's Pond** and **Coleman's Lake** are known throughout the state and are located within a mile or two of the town of **Midville**. Every year in April, Midville hosts a festival dedicated to that feisty game fish, *Lepomis Auritus,* better known as the **Redbreast** (www.redbreastfestival.org). The sweet, flaky, white flesh of this sunfish makes for excellent eating, especially fried after being dipped in seasoned cornmeal or pancake batter. Speaking of batter, I lived for a time in Midville (population 500) and served as its mayor. As it turned out, the game of politics wasn't my strong suit and I retired after a resounding re-election defeat. Oh well, it was probably for the best because it set me on the path that led me to this page and to you. Fate can be an odd thing you know. Besides my two fish camp favorites, there's also **Dye's Fish Camp** and **Peggy's Restaurant.** While not technically a fish camp, Peggy's is an example of the type of Sunday dinner-on-the-grounds and once-a-year Family Reunion cooking that every true Southerner knows and enjoys.

If taming the twisties is your only reason for riding then maybe this chapter isn't for you, but if good food and riding off the beaten path to interesting destinations rev your throttle, then you'll love these rides.

Trip 11 Middle Georgia's Fish Camp Tour

Distance *114 miles*
Terrain *Mostly flat to slightly twisty in parts, light to moderate traffic*
Highlights *Cypress pond, fish camps, roadside hand water pump, Georgia's first capitol, and smallest incorporated town*

This journey begins in a town made famous for a fraud. **Louisville,** named for King Louis XVI of France, is a sleepy farming town where I attended high school. I've included this route for two reasons. The first is to list the great restaurants in the area and the second is to fulfill a promise to a certain English teacher by the name of James P. Hight. I have to confess that I wasn't the best student during my years at Thomas Jefferson Academy, but I enjoyed high school. However, I didn't enjoy it enough to stay an extra year. When it began

Trees with knees. These cones are part of the pond-cypress root system which gathers oxygen during times of high water. These trees can grow to over 100 feet tall and live over 1000 years.

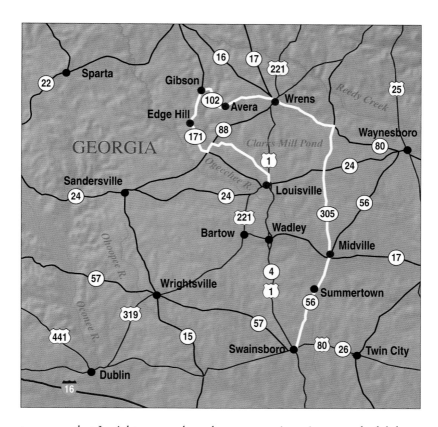

to appear that I might not graduate because certain assignments hadn't been turned in due to my mischievous dog which had a fondness for chewing assignment papers, I promised Mr. Hight that if he would allow me the opportunity to redo the paper, I would mention him in my first book. Promise fulfilled.

But that's not the fraud I was referring to. The **Yazoo Land Fraud of 1795** was an extremely complicated political scandal (aren't they all?). Yazoo makes the Clinton Arkansas Whitewater mess look simple by comparison. The condensed version is that after the Revolutionary War the state of Georgia encompassed what is today Alabama and Mississippi, some 35 million acres. Georgia did not have the resources to defend this territory and handle the issues between the Indian population and settlers moving west into these lands. So in 1795 the lands were sold to land speculation companies for roughly 1.5 cents per acre. The shareholders of these shell companies turned out to be Georgia politicians at the state and local level, newspaper editors, and other influential Georgians. The public cried fraud and the act was repealed and burned on the grounds by "fire from heaven." The "divine fire" was aided by a magnifying glass to heat some combustible material but that's a trivial detail. You can read about it on the historical marker located in front of the Neoclassical Revival style Jefferson County courthouse building in Louisville on East Broad Street downtown.

Another prominent landmark is the **Old Market House** at Mulberry Street and East Broad Street. During the depression, this historical building was partially renovated by members of the **Civilian Conservation Corp.**

There are several good restaurants in Louisville. **Pansy's** (203 East Broad Street, 478-625-3216) is open for breakfast and lunch. **Emily's** (401 West

THE ROUTE FROM LOUISVILLE

0	Start in downtown Louisville at Courthouse on East Broad Street
0.5	Turn right on US 1/SR 24 (Peachtree Street)
1.6	Bear left at Bypass and continue North on US 1
2.4	Turn left on Clarks Mill Road
7.8	Arrive at Clarks Mill Pond—Dye's Fish Camp
10.3	Turn left on Sand Valley Road
14.0	Turn left on SR 88
15.8	Turn left on SR 171
21.0	Enter town of Edgehill
21.1	Leave Edgehill
28.0	Turn right on SR 102
51.0	Hand water pump in Avera on left side of highway
59.0	Hwy 1/88/80 in Wrens and Peggy's Restaurant
60.3	Turn right on SR 80
72.0	Turn right on SR 305
94.7	Merge on SR 56 as SR 305 ends in Midville
95.6	Turn right on Wadley Coleman Lake Road
96.5	Turn right on Stevens Crossing Road. Retrace back to Wadley Coleman Lake Road. Turn left
97.5	Turn right on SR 56
99.0	(Optional) Turn left on Old Savannah Road to McKinney Pond Road 1.25 miles on left
113.0	Turn right on US 80/SR 56
113.7	Ride ends at US 1 and US 80 downtown Swainsboro

Before President Bill Clinton and the Whitewater Scandal there was the Yazoo Fraud and the tiny town of Louisville, Georgia, became famous because of it.

You won't find Edgehill, Georgia, on any of the recommended tourist destination maps, but it has the distinction of being the smallest incorporated town in Georgia. You could fit the entire population on a school bus and still have plenty of empty seats.

Broad Street, 478-625-0102) is open for lunch daily. Emily Fulghum also owns **Coleman's Lake Restaurant** (478-625-3216) that we'll visit at the end of our ride. When you're ready, head northwest on Main Street US 1 Business to Peachtree Street (SR 24) and turn right to continue on US 1 Business/SR 221.

At Mile 2.3, turn left on Clarks Mill Road. At Mile 7.7, you'll pass Clarks Mill Pond and our first Georgia fish camp. Unless you've started late or you happen to be on the right Sunday, **Dye's Fish Camp** (6595 Clarks Mill Road) will probably be closed. It is only open for dinner Thursday through Saturday 5:30 to 9:30 p.m. and the first and third Sunday of the month for lunch from 11 to 3 p.m. Located in a portion of the old grist mill, Dye's serves farm raised catfish and excellent fish camp style food. Nature lovers will recognize the trees in the pond as bald cypress trees. Relatives of the ancient redwoods and sequoias of California, bald cypress is a common sight in the South. This tree loves water and is distinguished by its "knees" which protrude from the roots out of the water. You should pull over and photograph the cypress and the Spanish moss hanging from its branches.

Continue north to Mile 10.3 and turn left on Sand Valley Road. At Mile 14.1, turn left on SR 88 and continue just under two miles and turn left on SR 171 toward the town of **Edgehill** which boasts of being the smallest incorporated town in Georgia. Here's an interesting note, if you bring two friends with you to visit, you'll have increased the town's population ten percent! With an official population of just 30 permanent residents, there isn't much to talk about but if you've come this far, take a photo of yourself standing in front of the "water" department which is a basic block pump house surrounded by a locked chain link fence. After all, this is post-911 and security of the water supply is paramount.

Continue north on SR 171 to the town of **Gibson** where you'll turn right on SR 102 and head toward **Avera.** Speaking of water, on the side of the road at Mile 34.6 is a shelter which houses an old hand pump. I've stopped at this pump several times on warm summer days for a cool refreshing drink of water brought up from mother earth. I'm not sure who looks after it but I sure do appreciate it!

Continue on SR 102 through **Stapleton** and into **Wrens.** At Mile 43.1, SR 102 intersects with US 1 and 88. Directly across the street is **Peggy's Restaurant** (101 North Main Street, 706-547-2111) which is open for breakfast, lunch, and dinner and serves delicious down-home southern style food. Owner Peggy Hadden is a charming example of southern manners who would have been at home entertaining guests in a spacious *Gone With The Wind* type mansion anywhere in the South. But, lunch at Peggy's is cafeteria style with ample portions. Be warned the tea is strong and very sweet. My daughter loves the macaroni, dressing, field peas, and butterbeans. Fried chicken is also served. You'll notice that just about every restaurant in the South with buffet or cafeteria style food features fried chicken on the menu. There's a reason for this, and I'll soon share it with you, but first, a little background on chicken.

It isn't the Fountain of Youth, but at least you won't have to "prime the pump" in Avera at this roadside well. Just start pumping the handle and you'll be rewarded with cool fresh water straight from mother earth. (Photo by Sylvia Cochran)

In the South, millions of dollars are generated every day from this humble fowl and hundreds of people depend on the bird for their paychecks. Fast food chains such as **Popeyes, Church's, and Mrs. Winters** dot the southern landscape. And let's not forget Col. Sanders and **Kentucky Fried Chicken**, that great southern institution that started it all.

There is hardly another food that unites and divides southerners more than fried chicken. Only barbeque rivals the yard bird in culinary controversy. The basic recipe for fried chicken is to coat a young tender skinned bird with a breaded mixture and fry or pan fry in oil. Variations are baked and pressure cooked. The divisions come from arguments over the best choices for breading and the best herbs and spices to use. Most of the recipes in use today began in a sharecropper or slave cabin where chicken was the basic staple meat and ways were found to enhance the flavor as much as possible with very few resources.

Okay, so chicken is a big thing, but why does almost every restaurant in the South serve fried chicken during lunch? Well because of the *Southern Food Police* of course. The SFP is a secret division of the *Order of the Southern Traditions.* We make routine inspections of lunch buffets all across the region to ensure that fried chicken will never disappear from the menu. Yes, I've been a member for years and take my responsibility seriously. You'll find me inspecting buffets all over the South to ensure the law is being upheld. My waistline

You're in Bulldog Country in Gibson, Georgia, at Usry's Diner. I can't vouch for the food because I've never had the opportunity to sample it, but I like their taste in football teams!

Neglected and fading into obscurity, this Revolutionary War-era graveyard in Jefferson County, Georgia, stands in mute testament to the harsh life our early forefathers endured. This photo shows the graves of 14 children who died before reaching their second birthday, all belonging to the same family.

has suffered, but it's a sacrifice I'm proud to make. The southern food police also inspect barbeque establishments for certain standards but according to policy, agents are limited to one food category. Back in the day before that rule was instituted we lost many good men who simply ate themselves to death doing their duty!

As you leave Peggy's, turn on SR 88/80 south toward **Keysville.** At Mile 61, turn right on SR 80, and ten miles later, turn right on SR 305 and continue south to Midville. **Midville,** like many small towns in the South was once a thriving community with a school and a bright future. Today Midville, while holding its own, is better known for the two competing fish camp restaurants a couple miles outside the city proper.

At Mile 95.9, turn right onto Wadley Coleman Lake Road and at Mile 97 turn onto Stevens Crossing Road which takes you to **Coleman's Lake Restaurant** (823 Stevens Crossing Road, 478-589-7726). Coleman's and nearby **McKinneys Pond Restaurant** (167 Mckinney Pond Road) are examples of traditional fishing camps that exist throughout the South. Located on the Ogeechee River, both restaurants serve sportsmen who visit to hunt in the area and fish in the river. Their private rooms have been used over the years by politicians, local preachers, and prominent citizens to enjoy good food and an

Southern Fried Yard Bird

My earliest food memory is watching the women in my life prepare fried chicken, and chicken fried steak. Good fried chicken starts out with the right bird. Young chickens, game hens, and fryers are the best choice. The rest is pretty simple.

You will need:

Chicken, pre-cut into legs, thighs, breasts, and back (if you don't know how)
1 brown paper sack
1 1/2 cups flour (adjust to amount of chicken to be fried)
1 tsp. salt per cup flour
4 tbs. bacon grease—saved from previous breakfast
Cooking oil (lard is preferred)
1 well-seasoned black iron skillet with cover

Wash the bird thoroughly but do not remove the skin. If you do, it's not southern fried chicken anymore. If you need a little variation from this recipe, it's acceptable to soak your bird overnight in buttermilk before you batter. Add the salt to the flour in the brown paper sack. Place each piece of chicken one at a time into the sack and shake well, making sure to cover the entire chicken. Add the bacon grease to the lard (cooking oil) and preheat the iron skillet to a temperature where the bird will fry slowly. If it fries too fast, you're going to burn the skin and undercook the flesh. You will add all your chicken and then cover the skillet, turning the chicken every few minutes until it is golden brown. Southern Fried Chicken is eaten with your fingers and served with mashed potatoes or cole slaw. Tastes best during Sunday dinner on the grounds.

* Chicken fried steak is prepared exactly the same except substitute well-tenderized (beaten to a pulp with a special type of hammer) cube steak. ∎

occasional adult beverage with their meals in privacy away from disapproving eyes. There's a local debate over which place serves the best food. Generally it's agreed that Coleman's has the edge for steaks and shrimp but McKinney's wins hands down on fish and coleslaw. Both are open Tuesday through Saturday for dinner only.

When you leave Coleman's Lake, retrace your route to Hwy 56 and at Mile 99.3, turn right and head toward Swainsboro. At Mile 100, you'll pass Old Savannah Road on your left. Turn here to visit McKinney's Pond and in 1.25 miles turn left again on the McKinney Pond Road. The restaurant is at the end of the road.

The Old Savannah Road intersects with this route near Wadley, Georgia, and runs by two fish camps near Midville.

At Mile 113, you'll arrive at the intersection of US 80 and SR 56. Turn right on US 80 to US 1. **Swainsboro's** nickname is "Where Main Streets Meet" because US 1 traverses the country from top to bottom, i.e., from Maine to Key West. US 80 once stretched from the east coast to the west coast, i.e., from California to Georgia. Today US 80 is broken up and you can no longer follow it the entire distance, but if you've a mind to, you can still ride US 1 the entire length.

Swainsboro is the end of our journey and where I began my career as a motorcycle author and publisher with *Dixie Rider*. In 2005 *Dixie Rider* changed names to *USRiderNews*. While you're in town I invite you to stop by ***USRiderNews*** (324 South Green Street, 478-237-3761) and I'll be happy to sign your copy of this book, or you can pick up a new copy for a friend or colleague. If you're hungry, there are a couple of good restaurants in town. **The Coleman House Bed and Breakfast** (323 North Main Street, 478-237-9100) serves lunch buffet from 11 to 2 p.m. Monday through Friday and on Sunday. The breaded and baked pineapple casserole is my favorite. They also serve excellent pork chops.

Trip 12   Exploring Georgia's Little Grand Canyon

Distance   *159 miles*

Terrain   *Two-lane road, straight with a few twists, well maintained asphalt. Traffic is light in the country, moderate in town.*

Highlights   *Railroad museums, authentic 1850s village, canyon views, hometown of a former President, and the airport where Lindbergh first flew solo*

We'll start this journey in the town of **Montezuma.** Just off I-75, this vibrant middle Georgia town was named by veterans returning from the **Spanish American War.** In fact the names of several towns on this journey were influenced by that war. Located at the confluence of **Beaver Creek** and the **Flint River,** downtown Montezuma was inundated with over six feet of brown

In a couple thousand years, Providence Canyon State Park near Lumpkin, Georgia, could be as world famous as the Grand Canyon, especially if the erosion continues.

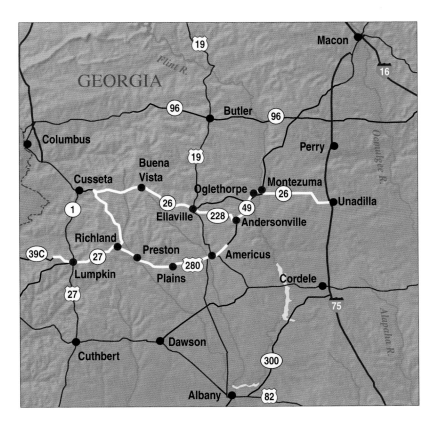

muddy water during the devastating floods of 1994. Right after the flood, the town started the **Beaver Creek Festival** to recognize those who worked so hard for the town's recovery and to mark the anniversary of the event. In the surrounding county is a large and thriving Mennonite community. Tourists come to **Yoder's Deitsch Haus** (GA Hwy 26 East, 478-472-2024), for one of the best lunches anywhere around. It's open from 11:30 to 2:30 p.m. Tuesday through Saturday and there is a bakery next door where you can fill your saddlebags with snacks for the days' journey.

When you leave Yoder's, head west to reach the city limits of Montezuma, and turn right at Mile 17 on Spaulding Street. You'll soon cross Beaver Creek. Remember that this seemingly harmless waterway flooded downtown with six feet of brown, muddy water which remained for six days. In less than one mile you'll reach East Railroad Street and directly in front of you is the **Montezuma Depot S. Dooley.** Built in 1890 and donated to the city in 1980, the depot was completely renovated in 2001 to 2002 and houses a railroad museum along with other shops. Across the street from the depot is the **Carnegie Library,** built in 1908 with a grant from the **Andrew Carnegie Foundation.** Carnegie was a wealthy industrialist who believed it was a disgrace to die wealthy. So he started giving away his money to build libraries. From 1881 to 1917 the man whose legacy was to become the free library gave grants in excess of $56 million dollars to build over 1,900 libraries in the United States and several hundred overseas. You might mistakenly believe that he really wanted his name immortalized in stone all over the country but he did not stipulate that any library be named for him. Instead his preference was to place a representation of the rays of the rising sun, and above it the words LET THERE BE LIGHT.

THE ROUTE FROM MONTEZUMA

0	Start on I-75 at SR 26
16.9	Turn right on Spaulding Drive
17.8	Cross Dooley Street to SR 49 (Oglethorpe Road) and continue to Andersonville Historic Site
27.5	Turn left into entrance of Andersonville POW Camp
29.3	Go straight across SR 49 to Church Street and downtown Andersonville Village
29.8	Turn left on SR 228
41.1	Turn right on US 19 in Ellaville
41.3	Turn left on SR 26
55.8	Go straight through Buena Vista across SR 41
67.5	Turn left on Liberty Hill Road
85.6	Turn right on US 280/SR 27
97.6	Turn right on US 27/SR 1
97.7	Turn left on SR 39C
105.0	Arrive at Providence Canyon
112.0	Turn right on US 27/SR 1
112.1	Turn left on SR 27 toward Richland
121.5	Go straight across SR 520 through Preston to Plains
139.8	Arrive in Plains
148.7	Turn left on US 19
149.6	Turn right on US 280/Forsythe Street West
151.0	Turn left on SR 49 toward Andersonville to Sumter Field
154.4	Turn left on Airport Road
159.0	Arrive at Lindbergh Monument

How many people pass this building daily without the slightest thought to the man who donated his fortune to erect storehouses of knowledge all over the world. Today the Carnegie Library in Montezuma houses the Chamber of Commerce.

From this intersection, pick up SR 49 toward **Oglethorpe** and continue on toward **Andersonville.** At Mile 27, turn left into **Andersonville National Historic Site.** Here you have a choice. You can continue straight on to the **National Prisoner of War Museum** and save the tour of the prison site and cemetery for later, or you can ride around the perimeter of the camp, take in

Unless you've lived through it, it's almost impossible to truly understand the mental and physical anguish that comes from being a prisoner of war. The POW museum at Andersonville, Georgia gives visitors a glimpse into that dark and desolate place.

These pieces of stone bear silent witness to the horrors of life and death as prisoners of war in Andersonville.

the monuments and read the historical markers, and then visit the active military graveyard and the museum. Either way, give yourself an hour or two to explore here. The Civil War buff will be familiar with Andersonville and the story of the camp. Known officially as *Camp Sumter,* it was built to house 10,000 captured Union prisoners but due to numerous factors came to house over 45,000. Of that number, 13,000 died due to unsanitary living conditions, poor medical care, and too little to eat. The commandant, Captain **Henry Wirz,** was made the scapegoat for conditions he was powerless to influence or change. Even though there were camps in the north, such as the one at Elmira, New York, which were as bad as Sumter, Wirz was the only person tried for war crimes. He was eventually hanged for mistreating his prisoners.

As you exit the park, you can continue straight across Hwy 49 into the old village. There is a seven acre pioneer farm complex, which includes a restored turn-of-the-century train depot and stores with Civil War memorabilia.

Dominating downtown is a monument to Captain Wirz. It was erected by the local community to honor the memory of a man who refused a pardon because its conditions would force him to sign a statement implicating others such as **General Robert E. Lee** or the President of the Confederacy, **Jefferson Davis.** Wirz is an example of the character of the men who fought with honor and died with dignity in that great struggle, and the memory of their sacrifice still resonates through the small towns of the South.

When you're ready to leave, continue on Church Street past the Wirz monument to Hwy 228. At Mile 30, turn left onto 228 and head west. This is my second favorite stretch of highway on this journey, as the road bends and twists just enough to keep you from being bored. Too soon you'll arrive in **Ellaville.** At Mile 41, turn right onto US 19 and in .2 mile (about one block) turn back left on SR 26. The next 13 miles are similar to the previous 11. Remain on SR 26 through **Buena Vista,** a town with a Spanish influence. It was originally named Taylor and then called Pea Ridge. In 1847, when word of a major victory in the Spanish American War near the village of Buena Vista, Mexico, reached the townsfolk, they chose to adopt this name for the town.

Continue west to Mile 67.4 and turn left on SR 26 toward the town of **Cusseta.** In approximately seven miles you'll cross a bridge over railroad tracks and at Mile 66.9, turn left onto **Liberty Hill Road.** Soon you'll understand why I

The town of Andersonville sits directly across the street from the museum and camp. It's worthy of stopping in and visiting the monument to Captain Wirtz.

Westville is a town that never was, but exists today as a time capsule dating back to the pre-Civil War-era of the 1850s.

took you on this little two-lane odyssey. The only negative about this road is the choice of paving material. I would prefer asphalt but the road is constructed with longer lasting composite material, gravel overlaid with asphalt packed solid. It's no problem to ride, but it's not as smooth as solid blacktop. In a few miles you'll make a sharp right to remain on the pavement but then continue straight as you notice the road name changes to Seminole Road. In a few miles you'll deadend at US 280/SR 27. Turn right and head through the town of **Richland** to **Lumpkin.**

In Lumpkin visit **Westville** (1850 Martin Luther King Jr. Drive, www.westville.org), an old town that is, but never actually was. Westville is a working 1850s town, recreated entirely to preserve the traditions of antebellum west Georgia in the period immediately preceding the Civil War. **John Word West** was a history teacher who had a passion to preserve the area's history for posterity and in 1928, began to collect nineteenth century buildings and artifacts. West corresponded with oil tycoon and philanthropist **John D. Rockefeller Jr.,** who had begun Colonial Williamsburg in Virginia about that time, and also with automotive pioneer **Henry Ford,** who founded Greenfield Village in Michigan. West died in 1961 and did not live to see his village come to life. However, the work he started culminated when **Governor Lester Maddox** presided over the village's formal founding on August 31, 1968. In

Westville you'll find over 30 authentically furnished Pre-Civil war buildings. For the best experience, visit either during the Spring Festival in mid-April or the Harvest Festival in late October and early November. During those times Westville comes alive with volunteers in period costumes performing traditional community activities, such as candle and shoe making, blacksmithing, and, my favorite, ginning cotton. I guarantee you'll come away with a better understanding of the South after this visit. Westville is open 10 to 5 April through January, Tuesday through Saturday except New Years Day, Thanksgiving, Christmas Eve, and Christmas. January to March call for times.

After leaving Westville, return to Main Street and turn left at the **Singer Co,** established in 1838, which lays claim to being Georgia's oldest working hardware store. It is showing its years, but if you remember old rolling ladders, wood floors, and buck knives you'll enjoy browsing. A few stores further up is **Dr. Hatchett's Drug Store Museum & Soda Fountain,** a time capsule just waiting to be opened. Dr. J. Marion Hatchett, a surgeon during the Civil War, opened the store in nearby Ft. Gaines in the 1870s and ran it until his death in 1894. Then his son, Samuel "Pope" Hatchett, took it over for 63 years until his death in 1957. Pope's widow locked the store and the entire collection and kept it exactly as it was at his death. When the town of Lumpkin restored one of its buildings to an approximate facsimile of the Ft. Gaines store, the family moved

Years ago the cure was sometimes worse than the disease. The Dr. Hatchett Drug Store Museum and Soda Fountain contains a well preserved collection from a family of pharmacists dating back to the late 1800s. It is a rare glimpse back to a time when medicine was more mysterious and less scientific.

the entire collection here. The building houses an authentic display of pre-FDA medicines and remedies commonly referred to as "snake-oils." You'll find products with names such as "666 Malarial Preparation," and "Pigeon's Milk," which turns out to be an entire kit for the treatment of gonorrhea. If you're waiting for the punch line, I'm not going there. If you're interested you can contact Allen Vegotsky (770-270-1034) who has inventoried the entire collection.

When you're ready to continue, head west on SR 27 to US 1. Turn right for a couple hundred yards and turn left on SR 39C toward **Providence Canyon State Park.** Providence Canyon is also known as **Georgia's Little Grand Canyon.** Called one of **Georgia's Seven Wonders,** Providence Canyon is a direct result of the poor farming practices of the 1800s. The settlers in the area had no understanding of soil conservation and simply plowed the land in the easiest manner, straight up and down the hills. Once the crops were harvested, the winter rains soon turned plow rows into ditches which evolved into gullies. In the blink of a geological eye, they have become massive ravines, the largest of which are over 150 feet deep! The result is a natural and unpolished tourist attraction. At one time enterprising locals tried to slow the pace of erosion by introducing non-native species such as kudzu and other ground covers but it has only been marginally successful. Even the steep quarter-mile trail from the interpretive center to the floor of the canyon is under constant threat of erosion. While this trail isn't for someone with a heart condition, I walked it in Sidi riding boots carrying a heavy camera bag—and I've sat behind a computer screen long enough to be pretty well out of shape. It didn't kill me, but I'm not making any promises. If you have the time, I do recommend the hike to the bottom, where you should turn left and head north into the canyon for the best views. This park isn't as busy as State Parks go and during certain times of the year you may enjoy it all to yourself. I don't recommend walking to the bottom after a rain shower or any time the ground is damp because of the sticky, slick red Georgia clay. To view the canyon from the rim, park in one of the spaces before you reach the interpretive center, and walk to the wooden fence. There are sections where you can stand within five feet of the edge. Remember, however, that the canyon is, in many places, still eroding and some of the ground will be unstable after a heavy rain. This is a changing landmark and the view you see today won't be the same one you will see if you return in a few years. Whichever you choose, treat our natural treasures with respect; take only photos and memories, and leave only footprints.

When you've had your fill of Little Grand Canyon, retrace your route to Lumpkin on SR 39C. At Mile 127, turn right on US 1 and immediately turn left again on SR 27. Stay on SR 27 through the town of Preston to Plains (www.plainsgeorgia.com).

In 1977 the world came to know a peanut farmer from this tiny southwestern town as Jimmy Carter, the 39th President of the United States. You'll find the town and its residents haven't changed much in the years since.

At Mile 138, as you enter the town of **Plains,** you'll pass a wooden guard house at Woodland Drive. This is the current home of the **39th President, James "Jimmy" Carter,** and **First Lady, Rosalynn Carter.** There is a viewing area but nowhere to park, so pull off on the other side of the road in a driveway and walk back across the highway. Luckily there isn't much traffic in this town of less than 1,000 residents. You'll notice a high black fence that surrounds the home and grounds as access to Woodland Drive is restricted by the Secret Service. It's easy to see that our former President is the favorite son of Plains; downtown there are several memorials to his accomplishments. During his Presidency, the media often enjoyed casting him as a rural hick and attempted to use his brother as proof. Billy enjoyed the spotlight, however, and often held court at his service station, which still stands next to the police station. Pull in and have your photo taken next to the sign. President Carter also had two sisters. Both are now deceased. One was a prominent evangelist, Ruth Carter Stapleton, and the other was Gloria Carter Spann, who was well known as an avid motorcycle enthusiast. Spann is buried in the Lebanon Church Cemetery near Plains and on her tombstone is the inscription "She rides in Harley Heaven." If you visit, leave a penny on the grave. There are several shops downtown that cater to the tourists traveling through and if you have a few minutes to spare you might want to stop in and purchase a souvenir or two.

Leaving a Penny on a Grave

There are several differences of opinion as to why people leave coins on graves. It started on Ben Franklin's tomb because of his "penny saved, penny earned" quote. I doubt it spread from that, but one theory goes back to the coins left with the dead in ancient Greece to pay Charon, ferryman over the River Styx—the price of transport to the Underworld. Another is the Jewish tradition of putting a small rock on the gravestone to mark one's visit, and that it's been changed in our culture of using small coins. Some even say that loved ones do it as a "penny for your thoughts" or "pennies from heaven" type of symbolism. I do it simply to pay respect and to leave something of mine in remembrance. It's kind of silly, but it does show that the deceased isn't completely forgotten by the living. ∎

Railroad buffs will want to time their schedule to coincide with the arrival of the SAM's Shortline. SAM stands for **Savannah, Atlanta, and Montgomery Railroad Company** which owned this line during the 1800s. Today it's operated by the **Georgia Department of Natural Resources** and the route runs between **Cordele** and **Archery,** Georgia, a distance of approximately 34 miles one way. Day trips usually depart Cordele at 9:30 a.m. and return by 5 p.m. For more information visit www.samshortline.com or call 877-GA-RAILS.

As you leave Plains on 27/280, you'll pass the **Plains Welcome Center.** You can stop in for more information on the area, the SAMS Shortline, and the special Amtrak train called the "Peanut Special" that departed from Plains after Carter won the election carrying friends and supporters to his inauguration in Washington, D.C.

At Mile 146, you'll enter the town of **Americus.** This is the end of our journey but there is still one more sight to see. At Mile 150, turn left onto SR 49 and head north for four miles to **Souther Field.** Turn left into the driveway and there at the terminal stands a monument to **Charles Lindbergh** who took his first solo flight over the cotton fields of south Georgia. Lindbergh had come to Americus because there was an abundance of affordable surplus WWI planes. He chose a Curtiss JN4 "Jenny" with a brand-new engine, a fresh coat of paint, and an extra 20 gallon fuel tank and paid just $500 for it. Although he only had 20 hours of flight instruction and had never flown solo, Lindbergh set off in May 1923 on a course that would change aviation history forever, and it started right here! Return to Americus and our journey's end. If you're hungry,

In a field near a rural south Georgia airport stands a monument to Charles A. Lindberg, who started his path to aviation history near the town of Americus where he made his first ever solo flight.

be sure to visit **The Station** (222 West Lamar Street, 229-931-5398) which is open Tuesday through Friday for lunch 11:30 to 2 p.m. If you're adventurous, try the fried cheese grits as an appetizer or with your meal; for dessert the creme brule is scrumptious. Across the street is the **Windsor Hotel Grand Dining Room** (West Lamar Street, 229-924-1555) which serves a buffet lunch and dinner Monday through Saturday. It's a tad sophisticated for the average motorcycle traveler so wear the clean leather and scrape the bugs off your teeth before you sit down. If you're still in town for breakfast or lunch the next day, try **Granny's Kitchen** at Hwy 19 and 280 (heading toward Plains). Prices are per entree or side dish, and the banana pudding is authentically delicious. It's open Monday through Saturday 6 to 2 p.m.

Trip 13   Georgia's Guidestones

Distance *130 miles*

Terrain *Well-maintained, two-lane blacktop, mostly flat with few demanding curves to distract you*

Highlights *Mysterious stone obelisks, monument to leather making, and museum to the greatest baseball player of all time. If you're interested in taking a three day cruise, this journey can be coupled with two rides in the South Carolina chapter, the Stumphouse Mountain ride and the Hail Ceasar Ride. You can easily do all three in a long weekend, and you'll return to work refreshed and ready to rejoin the rat race. Plus it beats the heck out of cutting the grass, cleaning the gutters, or those home improvement projects your spouse might have in mind for you!*

This journey begins at the intersection of Interstate 20 and SR 17 in **Thomson.** Reset your odometer as you cross the interstate. In 2.3 miles you'll turn right onto SR 43 and at Mile 15.3, turn right again onto SR 220. At Mile 18.5, turn left on Leathersville Road and pass through a settlement all but forgotten to history. In 1801, **Dr. John Bentley** established a tannery a few hundred yards from this spot and provided an essential service to the settlers in the

In 1980 these granite stones were unveiled to the public. The capstone inscription reads "Let These Be Guidestones to An Age of Reason."

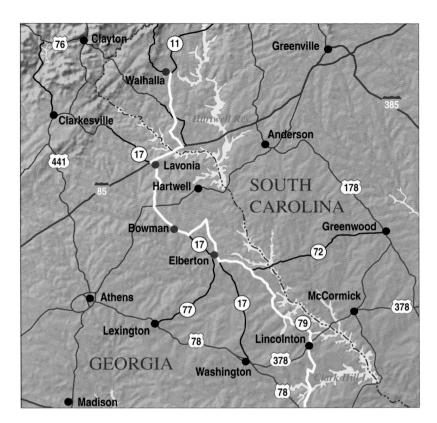

area. It's a stretch to take you several miles out of the way to see a granite monument to a vanished settlement but it's LEATHER! Think where we motorcyclists would be without those who kept the art of tanning leather alive. Leather is our friend and we should pay homage at every opportunity.

Continue on Leathersville Road for 4.5 miles. Turn right on SR 43 for 2.5 miles into **Lincolnton**, turn right on US 378 for a quarter of a mile, and then left on SR 79 for 27 miles headed to **Elberton**. At Mile 52.5, merge left with SR 72 and at Mile 61, turn right to merge with SR 17. At Mile 63.1, turn right onto SR 77.

Nine miles from downtown Elberton's intersection of SR 17 and SR 77 stands a six piece granite monument called the **Georgia Guidestones** (www.thegeorgiaguidestones.com). Quietly unveiled on March 22, 1980, this roadside oddity has been likened to England's Stonehenge and has been called **America's Rosetta Stone.** Reviled by some local religious groups and revered by others, this enigmatic structure sitting in the middle of what was once a cow pasture is shrouded in intentional and carefully planned mystery. Very little is publicly known about the person or persons who financed this site because they went to great pains to obscure their identity. It is known that the actual stones were quarried nearby, engraved and finished by Elberton Granite Finishing Company, Inc. at the direction of a man who identified himself only as R.C. Christian. But, Christian wasn't even his real name; he told everyone he

THE ROUTE FROM THOMSON

0	Start on I-20 at Routes 17/78/10
2.3	Turn right onto SR 43 (Lincolnton Road)
15.3	Turn right onto SR 220
18.5	Turn left on Leathersville Road
23.0	Turn right on SR 43 (Thomson Hwy)
25.5	Turn right on US 378
25.7	Turn left on SR 79 (Elberton Hwy)
52.8	Turn left on SR 72
61.4	Turn right on SR 17
63.1	Turn right on SR 77 (Hartwell Highway)
72.2	Turn right on Guidestones Road
72.5	Cross SR 77 heading east on Red Hill Road
73.1	Turn left on Maple Springs Road
75.0	Join Floyd Road and continue straight
77.0	Turn right on Pullam Mill Road
77.3	Turn left on Horse Farm Road
78.5	Turn right on Hard Cash Road
78.8	Turn right on SR 17 (Bowman Highway)
88.8	Turn right and merge onto SR 281/SR 17
89.2	Turn left on Cook Street
89.6	Arrive at Ty Cobb Museum in the Joe Adams Professional Building. (Turn Left on Cook Street out of the parking lot and turn right onto Cobb Memorial Street to exit)
89.8	Turn right on US 29/SR 8
90.0	Turn left on Bowersville Street at red light
90.4	Pick up SR 17 to Bowersville
103.5	Go through Lavonia to I-85 and turn left to head east
109.7	Exit on SR 11
129.6	Turn left on SR 28 to Walhalla, South Carolina

SITE OF OLD TANNERY

ESTABLISHED IN 1801 AT THE BALAAM BENTLEY
HOMEPLACE IN THE COMMUNITY OF LEATHERSVILLE
LINCOLN COUNTY GEORGIA

THIS MARKER IS PLACED ON THE ROADSIDE
300 YARDS FROM THE ORIGINAL HOMEPLACE
AND CEMETERY

ERECTED BY THE FORT JAMES CHAPTER
GEORGIA DIVISION, NATIONAL SOCIETY
COLONIAL DAMES XVII CENTURY

NOVEMBER 9, 2002

Where would we be without the humble hide of the cow? This monument stands to commemorate a tannery that was vital to the settlers of this area.

chose that name for himself because of his personal beliefs. He also said he represented a group of conservation-minded loyal Americans living outside Georgia who had been planning this monument for years. Christian had specific requirements for the site and one was that it be far from any major tourist areas. The location chosen affords unobstructed views of the rising and setting sun and is very close to what the Cherokees called "Al-yeh-li A lo-Hee," meaning The Center of the World. The six granite slabs form a paddlewheel type arrangement with one center stone called **The Gnomen Stone** surrounded by four stones and one capstone. In the Gnomen stone are astrologically aligned holes for viewing the sun and the north star. The four radiating stones are oriented toward specific points of the moon's annual rotation around the Earth. The capstone has a hole that functions as a sundial, marking the time of day and passage of the season. Engraved on each side of the four upright monoliths are ten edicts written in the eight major languages of the world: English, Spanish, Hindu, Hebrew, Arabic, Swahili, Chinese, and Russian. The inscriptions read:

The creators of the Georgia Guidestones went to great pains to hide their identity, but their new age message, engraved upon these granite slabs, is written in eight different languages.

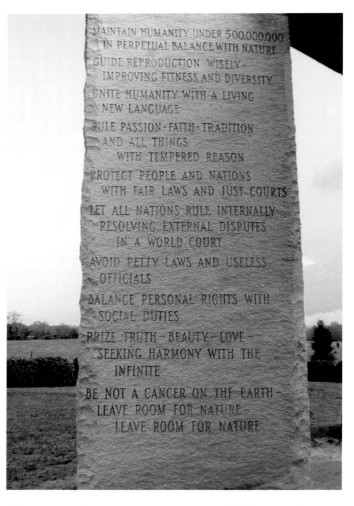

Maintain humanity under 500,000,000 in perpetual balance with nature. (With a current world population of 6.5 billion people, this one's going to be difficult to attain) *Guide reproduction wisely—improving fitness and diversity. Unite humanity with a living new language. Rule Passion—Faith—Tradition— and all things with tempered reason. Protect people and nations with fair laws and just courts. Let all nations rule internally resolving external disputes in a world court. Avoid petty laws and useless officials. Balance personal rights with social du- ties. Prize truth—beauty—love—seeking harmony with the infinite. Be not a can- cer on the earth—Leave room for nature—Leave room for nature.*

The capstone's inscription reads, "Let These Be Guidestones to An Age of Reason"

On a slab a few feet away is engraved all the technical and historical data pertaining to the stones and a message that a time capsule is buried beneath the slab with the date and time of its opening left purposely blank. Are these stones an obituary to our decaying civilization? Are they designed to guide the future of man in the event of nuclear holocaust? Or are they a cleverly disguised tourist draw meant to be shrouded in mystery? In a hundred years or so, will pilgrims flock to Georgia from all over the world in the same manner as today's tourists visit the Plains of Salisbury to view Stonehenge? I don't know, but it's worth the time to take the side trip to judge for yourself. To learn more about the Guidestones, visit **Elberton Granite Museum** where the admission is free and the hours are 2 to 5 p.m. Monday through Saturday.

Leaving the enigmatic guidestones behind, cross SR 77 heading west on Red Hill Road. Travel half a mile to Maple Springs Road and turn left. At Mile 75, stay on Floyd Road 1.8 miles to Pullam Mill Road where you'll turn right for a short .3 mile and then turn back left on Horse Farm Road. One mile later turn right on Hard Cash Road and in a few hundred feet merge with SR 17 again. Turn right and continue toward the towns of **Bowman** and **Royston.** Continue through Bowman and at 88.8 pick up SR 281 and 17 to Royston.

At Mile 89, turn left on Cook Street and in under a mile you'll come to the **Ty Cobb Museum** in the **Joe A. Adams Professional Building** (461 Cook Street, 706-245-1825). You will undoubtedly pause and think that a baseball

It might seem odd to you that a museum to one of baseball's greatest players of all time should share space with a medical office building. Once inside you'll learn the connection between Cobb and the medical community in this small Georgia town.

The traffic signals are electronic and the streetlamps are brighter, but the simple way of life can still be found in Royston, Georgia, the boyhood home of baseball legend, Ty Cobb.

museum in a medical professional building is a bit odd, but considering that this famous Georgia baseball player donated $100,000 to build the **Cobb Memorial Hospital,** I would deem the museum location most proper and fitting. It is open Monday through Friday 9 to 4 p.m., and Saturday 10 to 4 p.m., but closed most major holidays. Admission is $5 for adults and $4 for Seniors. Active military are admitted free.

When you leave the museum parking lot, turn left on Cook Street and then make an immediate right on Cobb Memorial Street for a tenth of a mile to US 29 and turn right. In less than half a mile, turn left on Bowersville Road in downtown at the Ty Cobb mural. In a few hundred feet, intersect with SR 17 and continue on through **Lavonia.** At Mile 103, you'll take the on-ramp to I-85 and head east across the northernmost section of **Lake Hartwell.** The lake was created in March 1962 when the **Corps of Engineers** built a dam across the **Savannah River** for electrical generation and flood control at a total cost of 89.2 million dollars. This dam and the dam at Clarks Hill are estimated to have prevented untold millions in property damage that would have been caused by periodic flooding.

At Mile 110, you'll turn right as you take the exit to SR 11. Turn left on the **Cherokee Foothills Scenic Highway.** After a few miles of seeing nothing more scenic than burned or rusting automobiles resting on concrete blocks in the yards of dilapidated mobile homes, you may start questioning the sanity of the person in charge of naming roads for South Carolina's DOT. This section of SR 11 is—uh, how can I say it diplomatically—*butt ugly*. Is someone playing a joke on the motoring public? Cherokee were the first settlers to this area so technically the designation is correct, but, scenic is a stretch. Yet, there are enough sites on or near the route to make it worth riding.

Continue on SR 11 to Mile 129.6. Turn left on SR 28 and in just over a mile you'll enter the town of **Walhalla** proper. Wallaha comes from Scandinavian mythology and means "Garden of the Gods" or "Valley of the Gods" depending on who you talk to. Its pronunciation is mighty close to Valhalla which in Norse mythology means "Hall of The Slain." But, I didn't want to start an argument with the local historical society so I didn't press the issue.

Known as the "Georgia Peach," Ty Cobb was considered by many to be the greatest all-around baseball player to have played the game. His business acumen and frugal living enabled him to amass a modest fortune of which he donated a large portion to improve the quality of life in rural Georgia.

Ty Cobb, The Georgia Peach

Tyrus Ramond Cobb, called "Ty," was born December 18, 1886 and started playing baseball before it became the civilized sport it is today. In the museum dedicated to his career at Royston, there is a short movie narrated by another famous sports figure in Georgia, **Larry Munson,** the voice of **Georgia Bulldogs Football.** Cobb still holds the highest lifetime major league batting average in history of .367. He was baseball's first inductee into its Hall of Fame, garnering more votes that year than even the famous Babe Ruth. Baseball fans will appreciate the significance that in his first 13 years as a major league player, Cobb won 12 batting titles. Some of the records he still holds are: most times stolen home (50), most times stolen all the way home from first base (4), most years played by an outfielder (24) and most errors by an outfielder (271, which is the American League Record), Casey Stengel once said of Cobb, "I never saw anyone like Ty Cobb. No one even came close to him as the greatest all-time player. That guy was superhuman, amazing."

Besides his prowess on the diamond, Cobb was a shrewd businessman, and wisely invested money he received for endorsements by purchasing stocks in growing companies. Cobb was a spokesman for another homegrown Georgia legend, Coca-Cola. While his salary never exceeded $40,000 a year, Cobb retired a multi-millionaire and lived out his retirement in Royston, shunning publicity. He earmarked 25 percent of his significant estate to fund the Cobb Scholarship Fund which helps send 100 Georgians to college each year.   ∎

Established in the mid 1800s on 17,859 acres purchased by the **German Colonization Society of Charleston,** the town soon became a well-known German Colony. Each year the town celebrates its heritage with a grand *Oktoberfest!* Several good restaurants in town stand ready to slake your hunger. The **Varsity Sandwich Shop** (193 Highlands Highway) comes highly recommended and the **Steak House Cafeteria** (316 East Main Street) has good, traditional southern fare. On SR 183 is the **Mountain View Restaurant** (1402 North Catherine Street) and as you enter town, **The Kuntry Kupboard,** (3708A Blue Ridge Boulevard).

Before you bed down for the evening, you might want to visit the **Confederate Memorial** that is pictured on the cover of this book. It's located in the center median near the edge of town on West Main Street. And, if you want to

Tyrus Ramond Cobb still holds the highest major league lifetime batting average of .367 and batted over .400 three times in his career.

know more about the meaning and controversy of the confederate flag, see page 250 of this book.

And, speaking of sleep, If lodging with local flavor suits you, then check out the **Liberty Lodge** (105 Liberty Lane, 864-638-8239), a nice bed-and-breakfast. Just back up the road a piece is the **Fieldstone Farm Inn Historic Bed and Breakfast** (640 Fieldstone Farm Road, Westminster, 877-835-2535, 864-882-5651). Besides the rooms in the house, there is a cabin and pool-side cottage to rent. Rates vary from $79 mid-week to $135 on the weekends.

If you're looking for chain type hotels, which I frequently am because I'm addicted to high-speed internet service, you may want to detour to **Seneca,** nine miles south on SR 28, where you'll find the **Best Western Executive Inn** (511 US Hwy 123 Bypass, 864-886-9646), **The Days Inn** (11015 Radio Station Road, 864-885-0710), and the **Jameson Inn** (226 Hi-Tech Road, 864-888-8300).

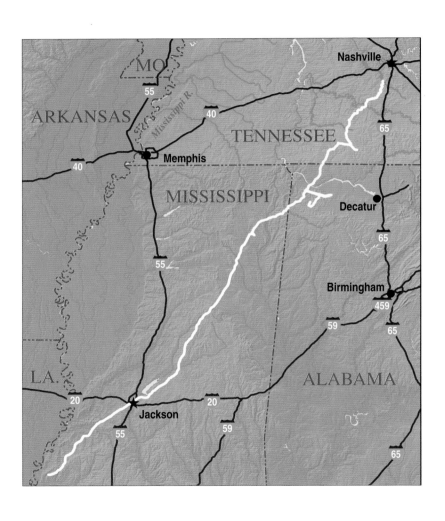

Natchez Trace Cruise

Where the Wild Buffalo and Indians Once Ruled

Before I discuss the Natchez Trace, here are a few words of caution. Watch for whitetail deer, especially in the early morning, evening, and night. During the rut season in the fall, the does will be quite unpredictable and the bucks will chase the does right into the path of your motorcycle, or any other vehicle, regardless of how loud your pipes are. Second, keep your speed below 50 mph. This is a national park and the "radar rangers" won't hesitate to give you a ticket.

This route through the wilderness was nothing more than a series of pig paths and buffalo trails that the native peoples used to traverse the region. The first recorded journey by a white man was an unknown Frenchman in 1742 who described the conditions on this trail as "miserable." The route became America's first "superhighway" in Colonial times between 1790 and 1830,

This overlook on the Ross Barnett Reservoir is a perfect spot to take a break and enjoy the setting sun before you reach Jackson, Mississippi.

For years McGee Castle hosted holiday celebrations, weddings, and was a unique bed-and-breakfast destination. Note the glass room on top of the tower on the right side of the photo.

mainly due to the fact that it was the only reliable and most expedient link between the goods of the North and the trading ports of Louisiana. The people of the Kentucky and Tennessee River valleys used the route to return from the markets in Natchez. Known as **Kaintucks,** these early entrepreneurs would build a flat boat, float down the Ohio, Cumberland, or Mississippi River to Natchez, sell the goods, and either break up the boat and sell it for lumber or just abandon it. Sometimes they might buy a horse for the return trip, but most times they just walked the 15 or 20 day journey up the 450 mile Trace. This was the most dangerous portion of the trip as the returning Kaintucks, their pockets bulging with cash, attracted all sorts of robbers and outlaws. Tales of travelers being robbed and murdered, then disemboweled and their body cavities filled with stones so the bodies could be submerged in some nameless creek, were told by those who used the route.

At one time the murder rate was so high the route earned the nickname of **"The Devil's Backbone."** Travelers soon learned to make the trip in groups for protection, often with the Postal Mail carrier. The official symbol of the Trace is a man astride a horse, which recognizes the importance of the letter carrier to the route.

By 1818 there were some 50 "Stands" or Inns in operation on the Trace, spaced roughly one day's walk apart. This helped lower the murder rate somewhat, but many a purse was stolen and traveler disappeared from a few of the less scrupulous Stand owners. The invention of the steamship eventually rendered the Trace obsolete. It was easier and safer to return up the river via steamboat and by 1830, the route was abandoned as an "official" highway, left to return to the wilderness from whence it was carved. As you travel along this paved replica, take the time to stop at some of the roadside exhibits and pause to reflect on what it must have been like for the traveler of the early 1800s, alone, and trying to get home with the meager pieces of gold earned in Natchez. The strangers you met in those days could just as well be a person who would murder you for what little you possessed. That puts our worrying about not having a strong enough cell phone signal in a whole new light, doesn't it?

I don't want to over hype the beauty of the **Natchez Trace** or give you unrealistic expectations. There are other routes in the South where the asphalt bends and twists around decreasing radius turns or opens up to sweeping views of breathtaking valleys with a kaleidoscope of changing fall colors. Don't expect that to happen here.

What you can expect is a byway filled with history and nearby towns with interesting and unusual things to see. For instance, you'll visit the final resting place of **Meriwether Lewis,** of **Lewis and Clark** fame, and the home of **David Crockett** of **Alamo** fame. Also, close by the Trace are the **Alabama Music Hall of Fame** and the birthplace of **W.C. Handy,** the father of the Blues.

In **Tuscumbia,** Alabama (www.tuscumbiaalabama.com), you'll have the opportunity to see where a little blind and deaf girl learned to communicate with the outside world to begin the journey that would take Helen Keller into history as the inspiration for disabled people around the world.

If you're a true-blue dyed-in-the-wool fan of the **King of Rock and Roll,** you will want to set aside plenty of time to spend in the place **Elvis Presley** was born, **Tupelo,** Mississippi. The museum at his boyhood home takes a couple of hours to see. While **Johnny's Drive-In** where Elvis went after school and on Saturdays is still operating, the most interesting site to me is **Tupelo Hardware,** where a clerk named **Forrest L. Bobo** changed the course of music history and sold Elvis his first guitar. True Elvis fans wouldn't miss any of this for the world!

There are also Civil War sites to see such as the **13 Unknown Confederate Soldiers** buried within walking distance of the Trace. History has lost the record of these brave souls but the Trace remembers. And speaking of burials, visit the famous **Coon Dog Cemetery** where Blue Tick, Red Bone, Black and Tan, and other coon dog royalty are buried.

The way to heaven is clearly illustrated by this gold-plated hand on top of the First Presbyterian Church of Port Gibson.

Within a stone's throw of the Trace stands **French Camp Academy Historic District** (www.frenchcamp.org, 662-547-6482) and the only bed-and-breakfast inn located directly on the Trace. Louis LeFleur established a stand here in 1812 and it became a school in 1822. The present Academy, built in 1885, long before the advent of public schools, was founded by a group of Scottish-Irish Christians to teach the youth of the area. Today the historic district has a log cabin museum and the **Council House Cafe,** which served as the official meeting place for Green LeFlore, the last chief of the Choctaw Indian Nation east of the Mississippi. Also on the grounds is the **Col. James Drane House,** a black smith shop, and a 1900s-era post office. Oh, and there's a bread bakery which claims to make the best homemade loaf in the state. I don't disagree!

As a short detour we'll leave the Trace and head west to **Vicksburg,** Mississippi, to see the history of the town painted on the murals near the mighty **Mississippi River.** We'll drop a few coins gambling on an authentic Mississippi river boat just like **Mark Twain** used to do, and (as old folks in the South say) I'll learn you something about the history of **Coca-Cola** that you probably thought you knew, but didn't.

I had planned to take you to **McGee's Castle** in Raymond (www.mcgeecastle.com), but the owner, William Dale McGee, unfortunately passed away just after my last visit and the castle has been closed with no word on any future events or tours. You can see the structure from the highway and hopefully it will reopen by the time you make your trip.

All too soon we'll arrive in **Natchez.** For me, my time spent on this highway is never enough, nor do I ever tire of its primitive beauty. After your journey along this ribbon of history, you'll have a better understanding of the soul of the **Natchez Trace Parkway** and I'll bet it will become one of your favorite roads, as it is mine.

One of the most enduring contributions of the American South to the culture of our nation has been the music of her native sons. The Alabama Music Hall of Fame commemorates those musicians who have helped shape the musical landscape of the past centuries.

Trip 14   Natchez Trace: Nashville to Tuscumbia

Distance   *182 miles*

Terrain   *Two-lane, well-maintained asphalt, uninterrupted by traffic signals or stop signs. Flat, moderate curves, easy to ride. Traffic is non-existent to moderate depending on the time and day. Avoid nighttime riding if possible due to abundance of wildlife.*

Highlights   *Relaxing two lane road, monuments to Meriwether Lewis and David Crockett, engineering bridge marvel, cemetery to coon dogs, and the river that earned a ferryman $75,000 in 1700!*

There are several approaches to riding the **Natchez Trace Parkway.** You can top off with gas at Mile 1 and ride as far as your tank will take you, without

When does a structure become more than just a collection of concrete and steel? I'm pretty sure the Natchez Trace Parkway Bridge has transcended its ingredients and now qualifies as a work of art.

stopping to see anything, repeating this each time when you get low on gas. This method will probably take you no more than one long day in the saddle. I've easily traveled 600 miles in a day on the interstate heading to Sturgis when my schedule demanded that I get there and back without delay. If that's your preferred method, then you've probably bought the wrong book. A good street atlas would have been more appropriate because that's not the type of journey I nor the other authors in this series promote.

The second approach is similar, but it does allow you to stop a few times during the day and read the roadside historical signs that explain the history of the Trace and the region this famous highway passes through. With this method you can probably complete this ride in two, or two and a half days. This is better than the first approach, but it's still not my favorite.

The third approach I call the "search and discover" motorcycle tour. The name is self-explanatory. There are numerous historical markers along the Trace, and the towns and byways near the Parkway contain enough charm and interesting sites that it would be a shame to ride blithely past without pausing to experience their uniqueness.

THE ROUTE FROM NASHVILLE

0   SR 100 at Natchez Trace Parkway

4.0   Natchez Trace Parkway Bridge

14.3   Turn on SR 46 toward Leipers Fork

14.9   Turn left to stay on SR 46 into town

17.1   Turn right on SR 46 toward Natchez Trace Parkway

18.0   Turn left on Parkway to head south

60.8   Turn right to Meriwether Lewis Memorial

62.0   Return to Trace and continue south

67.0   Turn left on SR 241 toward Lawrenceburg, Tennessee

73.5   Turn left at Stop sign where Route 241 merges with SR 240 for a hundred yards

73.7   Turn right to remain on SR 241

78.7   Turn left on US 64

84.7   Turn right on North Military Avenue to downtown Lawrenceburg

84.9   Return to US 64 and turn left

100.8 Turn left on ramp for Parkway to head south

129.0 Cross state line

151.0 Exit Trace on US 72

163.4 Turn right on SR 247

176.3 Turn right on Coondog Cemetery Road

182.0 Cemetery on left. Retrace route to SR 247, then turn left to US 72, and right on US 72 to Tuscumbia

Approaching the Trace in this manner will require a minimum of five days although it would be better to allow seven days to see and enjoy everything outlined in the next few chapters. Keep in mind that you always have the option to bypass any of these diversions and just continue on the Parkway. Since this is a linear route as opposed to the more circular routes used in the other chapters of this book, there is little or no chance to lose your way if you stick close to the Trace. You will have to leave the Parkway for fuel or refreshments when needed, but otherwise you can see as much or as little of the attractions outlined as you desire.

We begin this journey in **Nashville**, Tennessee. This portion of the Parkway has a 40 mph speed limit. It seems a little absurd, but who am I to question the wisdom of the National Park Service. In a few short miles the limit will increase to 50 mph, but a word of caution. The Park Rangers are serious about keeping speeders in check and during the height of the tourist season the chances are good that you will spot one of these Radar Rangers asking for a scofflaw's autograph.

There are a couple of good reasons for the lower than normal speed limit. First, there are no stoplights or stop signs on the Parkway, so while you might not think it, you can make very good time at 50 mph. Second, there is an abundance of wildlife in the wooded areas that surround the highway, and third, during the warmer months, the Parkway is a Mecca for bicyclists. Since the road doesn't have a wide paved shoulder, those under pedal power must share the road with the rest of us. The lower speed limit helps protect the "other" two wheelers!

As you proceed up the on-ramp to the Trace and drive over SR 100, you'll begin this 444 mile journey over a route once traveled by the wild buffalo, the **American Indian,** and **Andrew Jackson,** the country's seventh President. To claim that a spiritual ambiance exists on the Parkway might be a bit too poetic for the more pragmatic motorcyclist, but for those willing to believe, there is something transcendental about riding this ribbon of asphalt. It's not the overlooks or spectacular views that are common to the **Talladega Parkway** or the **Little River Canyon** run, on the **Natchez Trace,** there are extended stretches of continuous corridors of trees broken only by well-maintained pastoral settings. The lush forests and peaceful fields beckon you to relax, breathe deeply, and drink in the euphoric rhythm of two wheel travel on the Trace.

This modest structure was the home of a woman who dedicated her life to a deaf and blind child. The world remembers Helen Keller, but just as important to history was her selfless teacher, Anne Sullivan.

After just five miles you'll see **The Natchez Trace Parkway Bridge,** crossing over SR 96. This bridge was completed in 1996 and is one of only two post-tensioned, segmental concrete, arch bridges in the world. On your right is a pulloff named **Bird Song Hollow,** so take the time to stop. This is one of those spots where you can pull off and enjoy the view of this unique bridge before you ride across it. I know what you road warriors are thinking, "I just got started and now he wants me to pull off?"

At Mile 18.7, you'll exit to SR 46 and turn right to head into the town of Leipers Fork. In just under a mile, you'll turn left to stay on SR 46, and the intersection of Bailey Road with **Green's Grocery** on your right. Not to be confused with the modern convenience store across the street, Green's Grocery no longer sells hoop cheese and bologna as it once did, but it does occasionally serve up some delicious musicians who perform, informally. Directly across from Green's Grocery is an example of a hand dug well, and nearby are the authentic pre-Civil War slave quarters of an old plantation home.

For such a small village, **Leipers Fork** has quite a storied history. The area was settled in the late 1790s by pioneers who were given land grants as payment for their help in the Revolutionary War. Early travelers on the Trace referred to this area as **Bentonville,** so named for **Thomas Hart Benton,** who later became a U.S. Senator from the state of Missouri. The story of how he came to be in Missouri and the town renamed to Hillsboro, which later changed to Leipers Fork, is fascinating.

One of the Benton family members quarreled with **General Andrew Jackson** in nearby Nashville and during the resulting brawl, a gun was drawn and Jackson was shot in the shoulder. Because Jackson survived, the Bentons decided that Tennessee wasn't big enough for both families so the Bentons picked up and moved to Missouri. After they left, the townspeople decided to rename their village **Hillsboro,** since many of the remaining settlers had migrated from the area around Hillsborough, North Carolina. In the early 1800s a post office was established in the village because of its growth and its location on the Natchez Trace Parkway. However, the name Hillsboro was already being used by another town in Tennessee so the town adopted the name Leipers Fork, after a family who owned much of the land surrounding the creek that passes through the town.

Now that you've gotten your history lesson, you can enter into the town proper. Don't blink or you'll bypass the whole of downtown. Antiques are the name of the game in this village and while that doesn't usually interest the space-starved motorcyclist, the Ford Police cruiser, reminiscent of Mayberry and a genuine replica of the "General Lee" used in the television show *The Dukes of Hazzard,* is parked in the middle of town and are reason to pause and pose for a photograph or two. If you arrive hungry, **Puckett's Grocery** (615-791-6484) is a good spot and also occasionally hosts talented musicians. **The Backyard Cafe,** (615-790-4003) offers sandwiches, coffee, and desserts, and directly across the street is the **Country Boy Restaurant** (615-794-7680), a working man's establishment that serves the kind of food that sticks to your ribs, and around your waist. For breakfast, I like their western omelets and for lunch, their meat and two vegetable special is standard fare in the South and plenty filling.

Now retrace your route to the Natchez Trace and head south. Your next stop is the **Meriwether Lewis Memorial** near the Alabama line. At Mile 60.1, turn right at the well marked entrance to the location of this famous explorer's grave and memorial.

Leaving the park you'll return to the Parkway and continue south toward the town of **Lawrenceburg.** At Mile 66.1, turn left onto SR 241. In 6.6 miles, the highway deadends and you'll turn left to join SR 240 for a couple hundred yards. Past the convenience store, turn back to the right to stay on SR 241. In five miles at Mile 78, turn left on Routes 64/242 to ride six miles and arrive at the public square in Lawrenceburg. If you're hungry, **The Square 40 Restaurant** (40 Public Square, 931-762-2868) features simple southern cooking at reasonable prices. Across the street is **Sweets and Sodas** (12 Public Square, 931-762-7880) where the hamburgers are okay, but the cookies are nothing to write home about. For southern barbeque at its finest, there's **Big John's BBQ** (904 North Military Avenue, 931-762-6739). At the south entrance to the square stands a statue of **David Crockett.** Your history teacher may have called him Davey, but that's not how they refer to him in Lawrenceburg. You might remember passing a sign as you came into town pointing toward the **David Crockett State Park and Restaurant** (931-762-9408, open daily 7 a.m. until dark). Along the banks of **Shoal Creek,** in what is now his namesake park, Crockett established a powder mill, a gristmill, and a distillery, but he lost them all in the flood of 1821. This financial undoing set Crockett on the path that took him through Congress where his support of the Cherokee and his opposition to their removal eventually ruined him politically. That's when he headed west toward a little mission in Texas called the **Alamo.** Perhaps you've heard of it. To learn more about the Cherokee and David Crockett, visit the **Cherokee David Crockett Museum and Cultural Center** located in the Bank building on the north side of the Public Square. Lawrenceburg is also the birthplace of former State Senator and actor **Fred Thompson** of the television series *Law and Order* and who starred in such movies as the *Hunt for Red October* and *Die Hard II.*

Once you've had your fill of Lawrenceburg, leave town heading west on US 65 and drive for 15 miles before returning to the Parkway. From there you'll head south toward Florence, Muscle Shoals, and Tuscumbia, Alabama. Usually

Meriwether Lewis—Murder or Suicide?

The story of this man who became famous for mapping the first route to the Pacific Ocean ends on the Natchez Trace on October 11, 1809, at **Grinders Stand,** just five years after his completion of the **Lewis and Clarke expedition.** Lewis, who was only 35 years old and recently appointed Governor of the Louisiana Territory, was traveling to Washington to see the President to clear his name from accusations of poorly handling public funds. Lewis had been Jefferson's personal secretary before the President appointed him to co-lead the famous expedition with William Clark. The official account of his death is that early in the morning hours the inhabitants of Grinders Stand heard two gunshots, and **Meriwether Lewis** was found dead with one gunshot wound to the head and another to the chest. Some say it was suicide, despite the fact that the guns used were the muzzle loading type, and some say his political enemies did him in. Either way, the explorer was buried in the pioneer's cemetery near the Stand in an unmarked grave. Depending on the time of the year and the amount of visitor traffic, you may be able to take pause and listen to the crows call in the trees and fields surrounding the park. If you close your eyes their lonesome "caw, caw, caw" will readily conjure up visions of the 19th century explorer traveling through the wilderness, his soul weighted down with melancholy.

For almost four decades, Lewis's grave remained unmarked until the State of Tennessee in 1848 appropriated $500 for the current marker. You'll notice it appears to be broken at the top and you might be inclined to believe it to be the work of graveyard vandals. But, the broken monument was created deliberately "to denote the violent and untimely end of a bright and glorious career." In 1925 President **Calvin Coolidge** set aside this area as a Federal Park, and with the completion of the Natchez Trace, the gravesite of the famous explorer now receives thousands of visitors annually. As a side note of interest, fellow Corp of Discovery explorer **William Clark** lived to be 68 years old and is buried in his family plot in Bellefontaine Cemetery in St. Louis, Missouri.

On the monument is the inscription *Immaturus obi: sed tu felicior annos Vive meos, Bona Republica! Viva tuos,* which means "I died young: but thou, O Good Republic, live out my years for me with better fortune." President **Thomas Jefferson** is credited with providing those words for his friend and protege. On the site is an authentic log cabin moved here to serve as a museum and office. Sign the guest book and look for a January 2006 entry where the first public announcement of this book was written by my very hand. ∎

I always get a sense of melancholy whenever I visit the final resting place of Meriwether Lewis just off the Natchez Trace Parkway. It's as if the tortured spirit of that great explorer is still waiting for the day when the questions surrounding his untimely death will be answered and his name cleared.

I make this area my last stop for the day since there are several nice chain hotels and reasonable accommodations. There are, however, a few more sights to see before the day ends.

Before you cross the state line into Alabama, you'll come to a section of the original Natchez Trace which shows how it appeared to travelers in the early 1800s. Three side-by-side routes evolved to allow folks to avoid parts that would become impassable due to heavy wagon traffic. Pause for a few minutes and think about how difficult it was for pioneers and settlers to haul their belongings overland in wagons on terrain like this.

As you approach Florence, you'll have several opportunities to exit the Parkway. If you're in a hurry, SR 20 will cut off a few miles and take you straight into downtown **Florence,** but I recommend continuing south until you cross over the **Tennessee River** on the **John Coffee Memorial Bridge.** At just under a mile long, the view from your saddle as you ride across this bridge, especially in the late afternoon or early morning, is worth going a little out of your way. The first time I rode it, the traffic was light and the tranquility of the scene was so refreshing I turned around on the other side to ride across it again. At the

To coon dog owners, having their favorite hound's final resting place memorialized with a stone marker isn't the least bit odd.

Natchez Trace Mile Marker 327.3 is the historic site of **Colbert Ferry. George Colbert** once operated a stand (an inn) and ferry here and is reported to have charged Andrew Jackson, who was returning from the Battle of New Orleans, $75,000 to ferry his army across the river. Quite a princely sum in those days!

At Mile 150 you'll exit to the right and loop around to US 72. From here turn right at the convenience store and drive 11.7 miles to SR 247. In 12.8 miles, you'll turn right onto Coon Dog Graveyard Road. Like the road name implies, the attraction here is an oddity that I bet you won't find outside of the American South. The only coon dog graveyard that this author is aware of in the country is located just five miles after you turn off SR 247. The road isn't in the best of shape for motorcycle riding, but it is a nice road with a serious elevation change and curves that will leave you begging the county to resurface it. In about three miles you'll emerge at the top of the ridge with a view for several miles in either direction. At Mile 182, you'll come to the nondescript entrance to the **Freedom Hills Coon Dog Cemetery** on your left. Started in 1937 when Mr. Key Underwood chose this spot to bury his legendary coon dog Troop, this cemetery is well known to those who take coon dog hunting seriously. In fact every Labor Day the **Tennessee Valley Coon Hunters Association** celebrates in true southern style at what has been called the only "official" coon dog graveyard in the country. There are at least one hundred graves located in this wooded area, complete with a covered pavilion and genuine working outhouse.

Coon Dog Hunting

Coon hunting is pretty simple because the dogs, at least the good ones, do most of the work. These hounds, trained to follow the scent of the raccoon, are directly descended from the hounds used to locate escaped and missing persons. If you've ever seen movies where someone makes a break for it, usually from a work detail, and they bring out a handler with three or four dogs straining on the leash, baying a soulful barking sound, those are known as bloodhounds, and were brought to the U.S. from Europe. Coon dogs are the first cousins to these trackers and were bred and trained here. In case you ever find yourself in a conversation about the sport of coon hunting, knowing the breeds will allow you to converse intelligently about these hounds. The best ones are the pure breeds of Blue Tick, Red Bone, Black and Tan, Treeing Walker, English, and Plott coonhounds.

Now for the city dwellers among you, hunting defenseless animals with dogs might be barbaric and politically incorrect, but for generations of boys growing up in the American South, coon (raccoon) hunting was a rite of passage and a social convention that was passed down from grandfather to father to son. And don't think for a minute that the dogs always win. Raccoons are fierce fighters, as dexterous with their paws as a monkey, and excellent swimmers. Many a good hound has been drowned by a big coon when caught in a stream or pond. During hard times, coon skins and meat kept whole families from starving to death. Today there isn't much demand for the meat or pelts but the hunt still bonds men and boys to each other and to the land.

My favorite time to visit this spot is late on a summer afternoon, when the world quiets down and I can sit on one of the stone benches and imagine hearing an ole treeing walker hound as he picks up the scent of his quarry, baying somewhere miles away. There is no other sound like it. I leave before dark however as the trip back to Route 272 on this unmarked, rippled blacktop country road isn't the best choice for the motorcycle traveler.   ■

Turn back left onto 272 and reconnect with US 72. From here turn right and travel seven miles into Tuscumbia, Alabama. You have your choice of several good overnight accommodations in the towns of Tuscumbia, Florence, or Muscle Shoals.

Trip 15 Natchez Trace: Tuscumbia to Tupelo

Distance *77 miles*

Terrain *Two-lane, well-maintained asphalt, uninterrupted by traffic signals or stop signs. Flat, moderate curves, easy to ride. Traffic is non-existent to moderate depending on the time and day. Avoid nighttime riding if possible due to abundance of wildlife.*

Highlights *Two lane winding blacktop, historical sites such as Helen Keller birthplace, Palace Ice Cream shop, Elvis boyhood home*

At 13 years old, the future King of Rock and Roll isn't swiveling his hips, but in this bronze statue, located on the grounds of the Elvis Presley boyhood home and museum, he is carrying the instrument that would one day propel him to fame.

Today is a short-ride day. You'll only travel 64 miles of the Trace Parkway. Why the short day? I'm assuming that you'll want to start your day visiting some of the sights I've outlined in Tuscumbia and Florence, and end your day touring the King of Rock and Roll's boyhood home. Of course, you're welcome to skip any of these and continue on to Jackson. There are a couple of chapters that use Natchez, Mississippi, as a hub, so proceed at your own pace.

THE ROUTE FROM TUSCUMBIA

0	US 72A at US 43. Head west on US 72
20.3	Take on-ramp to Natchez Trace Parkway, head south
51.6	Historical Marker—Unknown Confederate Dead
65.0	Natchez Trace Parkway visitor center
77.0	US 78 in Tupelo

Tuscumbia and **Muscle Shoals** are on the south side of the **Tennessee River** and **Florence** is on the north side. This part of Alabama is well known for its contribution to the American music scene and is home to the **Alabama Music Hall of Fame** (www.alamhof.org, 800-239-AMHF), located on US 72 in Tuscumbia and open Monday through Saturday 9 to 5 p.m., closed on Sunday. Admission is adults $8, students (13 to 18) $7, seniors (55 and older) $7, children (6 to 12) $5, children (5 and under) free. It's worth an hour detour to visit especially if you love music and history, as I do. The Hall honors only those musicians with ties to Alabama and you will be surprised at who is enshrined there. Contemporary artists include **Jimmy Buffet** (surprise—he's from Mobile), **Lionel Richie** of The Commodores, **Toni Tennille** of the Captain and Tennille, and **Wilson Pickett**. Other notables are **Hank Williams** and **Jim Nabors,** who most of you remember as Gomer Pyle, but was an accomplished musician in his own right. The famous country group **Alabama** has one of their well-worn tour buses on display and visitors can walk through it. Of course, the father of the blues, **W.C. Handy,** has a display, since his boyhood home is just across the river in Florence. In the small log cabin which houses the **W.C. Handy Birthplace and Museum** (620 West College Street, 256-760-6434, hours Tuesday through Saturday 10 to 4 p.m., admission: adults $2, students $0.50) is an extensive collection of his personal papers and artifacts. Each November the town of Florence hosts the **W.C. Handy Music Festival** (www.wchandymusicfestival.org).

In the South as in many parts of the country our downtowns and courthouse squares have suffered from the rise of the big-box retailers. A consequence has been that many older buildings have been abandoned in favor of strip malls and easier parking. Unfortunately, this trend results in towns and cities without character, virtually indistinguishable from towns and cities of similar sizes everywhere else. One man in Tuscumbia has been fighting this trend for the past few years and his name is **Harvey Robbins.** Robbins has invested millions of dollars of his family's fortune in restoring downtown Tuscumbia partly out of love for his hometown and the soda fountain where he met his wife. The **Palace Ice Cream and Sandwich Shop** is located in the old **Railroad Hotel** built in 1833. The name was later changed to the **Major Pope Railroad Hotel** (256-386-8210, open Monday through Saturday 11 to 5 p.m. and Sunday 1 to 5 p.m.) and is located at the corner of Main Street and 5th Street. Less than two blocks from the railroad depot, the soda fountain was installed in the Palace in 1906 and became the place to hang out and meet friends in the early part of the last century. If you're hungry for local flavor, try the egg and olive sandwich, or the $2 banana and peanut butter sandwich. The chili cheese hot dog, bacon cheeseburger, and the cobbler a la mode are also popular, but will force you to loosen your belt a notch or two.

In addition to The Palace, Robbins Properties Inc, has completed other downtown renovation projects, most notably, **Spring Park**, located on Spring Park Road. Here, Robbins installed a 48 foot waterfall that looks so natural that you wouldn't know it wasn't always there if you weren't told. There's a kiddie train that circles the park, a huge wooden Indian carved with chainsaw, and, to lure visitors to downtown after dark, a water show with lighted fountains that shoot water 150 feet in the air and are choreographed to music. The spectacle routinely draws thousands on the weekends. Check the schedule before you travel because the fountain show is closed during the colder months.

But, as generous as he is, Harvey Robbins isn't Tuscumbia's most famous citizen. That honor is reserved for someone who has inspired millions of disabled persons all around the world—**Helen Keller. Ivy Green** (300 West North Commons, www.helenkellerbirthplace.org) is her childhood home,

A simple water pump stands as an enduring symbol of the strength and resiliency of the human spirit. With the help of her teacher, Anne Sullivan, it was here that Helen Keller first learned to communicate with a world that she could neither see nor hear.

located at the corner of Keller Lane and North Commons Street East. Admission is $6 for adults, seniors $5, and students 5 to 18 years old $2; tours are conducted daily and the last one starts at 3:45 p.m. On the grounds is the actual pump where the "miracle" took place between seven year old Keller and her teacher, **Anne Sullivan.** Keller was blind and deaf and at this pump, Sullivan spelled the word "water" repeatedly into the child's hand until the child understood and broke out of her world of darkness and silence. By the end of that first night, Helen had learned 30 new words. In 1904 Helen Keller became the first disabled person to graduate "cum laude" from prestigious **Radcliffe College.** Every year on the last full weekend in June the town hosts a festival honoring the woman who came to be known worldwide as the **First Lady of Courage** (www.wraygraphics.com/hkfest).

For food, you can sample the local flavor at **The Rocking Chair Restaurant** (814 Highway 72 West, 256-381-6105), serving good food in generous portions. **J Fiddler's Restaurant** (1606 Hwy 72 West, directly across from the Polaris/Victory Dealership, 256-314-5501) serves a $4.50 lunch special and on Tuesday night has the best fried catfish in North Alabama. If catfish isn't to your taste, there's also fried chicken or the country fried steak. J Fiddler's is a typical southern road-house but one without the alcohol. There's a little stage for the bands that play on the weekend providing good music for your dining pleasure. If more working class type fare is to your liking, head east on Hwy 72/

To learn all about the Natchez Trace, stop in at the brand new visitors center, opened in late 2006 near Tupelo.

The Natchez Trace is the longest interpretive museum in the United States. Its 444-mile route is dotted with wooden signs like this, which explain the historical significance of this early trade route.

20 to **Jody's Restaurant** located right beside **Arnold's Truck Stop** (1440 Highway 20 East, Tuscumbia, 256-389-9005). Owner JoAnn Hare slings a mean plate of grub, certified authentic southern style by legions of locals and 18-wheeling road warriors.

As you depart Tuscumbia, head west on 72/20 and return to the Parkway west of Cherokee. We won't be too concerned with mileage this trip because we'll end the day in **Tupelo,** Mississippi, and won't take any detours off the Parkway.

If you want, reset your odometer as you join the Trace and then head south. Since it's only 63 miles to Tupelo and the day's end, I'll let you decide the number of historic markers along the route you may want to stop at. I always find them fascinating to read and learn about the early Americans who used this wilderness highway, so I end up stopping at them all.

Twentymile Bottom overlook is one of my favorites. It is here that you'll find the description of the Trace written in 1812 by Reverend John Johnson.

One of history's mysteries lies a short five-minute walk off the Trace near Tupelo where you'll find these graves of thirteen unknown Confederate Soldiers.

I have this day swam my horse five times, bridged one creek, forded several others beside the swamp we had to wade through. At night we had a shower of rain; took up my usual lodging on the ground in company with several Indians.

Standing on this overlook you can understand how physically difficult this overland journey was for these early travelers.

If you're a Civil War buff, be sure to stop just north of Tupelo at the gravesite of the **13 Unknown Confederate Soldiers.** Park and walk the short distance along the original Trace to the 13 headstones. Curiously all the markers face away from the graves toward the Trace. Who were these soldiers? By the time the Civil War engulfed the country, the main parts of the Trace were no longer in use, but this section was sometimes used by the Confederates. There are no historical records telling us who these souls are, so their story is lost to the ages. My personal belief is that they were soldiers returning from the battle at **Brices Cross Roads,** but that's just my guess.

At Mile 45, you'll come to the **Natchez Trace Parkway Visitor Center** just outside of Tupelo. Newly restored, this center is an excellent place to stop and learn more about the history of the highway and gather brochures for your journey. We're going to end our journey in nearby Tupelo but you may want to continue on south. It's your choice.

If you continue into Tupelo, turn right at Mile 58.6 to exit the Trace at SR 178 McCullough Boulevard. Turn right at the bottom of the ramp and make a U turn a few feet up where the divided intersection ends, and head east into town. At Mile 63, you'll pass **Johnnie's Drive In** on your right. Depending on your love of all things Elvis, you might want to stop in and enjoy one of their hamburgers or cheeseburgers just like Elvis did when he was a boy. I really can't recommend the food on its own merit but I do find the place fascinating for the memorabilia on the walls. When you're finished, turn right for a few feet to Elvis Presley Drive and turn left. The boyhood home of the **King of Rock and Roll** with a museum and chapel is located at 306 Elvis Presley Drive. The home is modest by any standard and while the furniture isn't original, it is authentic to the time period. Elvis's father endorsed the layout. Hours are 9 to 5:30 p.m. on Monday through Saturday from May to September, 9 to 5 p.m. on Monday through Saturday from October to April, and 1 to 5 p.m. on Sunday year round, closed for Thanksgiving and Christmas. You have to buy a ticket in the museum to enter the home, but you can wander the grounds and visit the chapel without a ticket.

Inside Johnnie's Drive In is a booth that the owners claim was Elvis's favorite on his after school visits for a cheeseburger and a milkshake. Johnnie's is still serving milkshakes and cheeseburgers to aspiring rock stars in Tupelo.

Elvis' First Guitar

The story is that Elvis had his eye on a .22 rifle for his birthday but his momma, Gladys, wouldn't hear of it. She thought a guitar would make a more appropriate birthday present. So Forrest L. Bobo, a clerk at Tupelo Hardware Store, got one of the inexpensive guitars from his display and handed it to Elvis. There is a spot marked with a duct tape X on the floor where legend says Elvis stood as he strummed that guitar. The guitar cost $7.75 plus 2 percent sales tax and was probably a Kay brand although that detail has never been verified. In fact, by the time he recorded his first hit, the Tupelo Hardware Store guitar had vanished, most probably traded in or lost. Several other notable stars have also made the journey to Tupelo to purchase a guitar from the same store, including **Patty Lovelace,** and **Steven Tyler** from Aerosmith. In fact, the store sells hundreds of guitars a year along and thousands of t-shirts to busloads of tourists. It is fascinating that almost four decades since his death, the allure of Elvis is still this strong. ∎

Elvis fans will, no doubt, find the house and museum fascinating, but everyone should enjoy our next stop, **Tupelo Hardware Store** where Elvis first

Here is where Elvis Presley and his twin brother Jesse were brought into the world. Jesse was stillborn. Today this house is located on the grounds of the Elvis Presley Museum in East Tupelo, MIssissippi. A small admission fee is charged.

The Tupelo Hardware Store is where Gladys Presley bought her son Elvis his first guitar. Besides hardware items, the still working 1920s-era store sells hundreds of guitars to tourists, fans, and famous musicians each year.

picked up a guitar. When you leave Elvis' home turn right on Main Street and drive west for approximately one mile. **Tupelo Hardware Store** (www.tupelohardware.com) will be on your right. From the minute you pull up to the front of this store, you will be transported back in time. The window displays are reminiscent of the 1950s with red wagons, tools, and toys. Once you step through the doors, the interior is exactly as hardware stores all over the country appeared in the early part of the last century. From the creaky wooden floors, long wood-and-glass display cabinets, sliding wall ladders to the pounded tin ceiling tiles, the smell of the past reaches into you and will leave first-time visitors gawking at the sight. But remember, this is no museum; it's a working hardware store so don't get in the way of the paying customers. Fortunately, the owners, the Booth family, are used to Elvis fans and tourists and it probably won't be long before one of their long-time employees will offer to be your tour guide, so to speak.

Our journey ends here but you have the option to continue south along the Trace or continue exploring Tupelo.

Trip 16 Natchez Trace: Tupelo to Natchez

Distance *216 miles*

Terrain *Two-lane, well-maintained asphalt, uninterrupted by traffic signals or stop signs. Flat, moderate curves, easy to ride. Traffic is non-existent to moderate depending on the time and day. Avoid nighttime riding if possible due to abundance of wildlife.*

Highlights *Relaxing two lane travel, historic French settlement, Vicksburg Civil War history, first Coca-Cola bottling plant, authentic paddlewheel gambling boat, Mississippi crafts*

Today's journey begins where yesterday's ended in **Tupelo,** Mississippi. While we're covering 216 miles today, it shouldn't take you a long time because most of the day will be spent in the saddle. With only one recommended stop in French Camp, you can make good time. Where this plan falls through is when you wind up stopping at every interpretive marker on the Trace as I do! If that's the way you travel, then this route will take you all day. At days end, you have the option to spend the night in historic Vicksburg on the Mississippi River or continue to Natchez some 90 miles further south under the cover of darkness.

As you leave Tupelo and head south toward **Jackson,** the traffic on the Trace becomes notably less hectic and the pace more serene. Every so often you'll approach narrative historical markers which will give you insight to different

The only bed-and-breakfast inn located directly on the Trace is at French Camp, along with a historical display of life during the heyday of the Natchez Trace Parkway.

cultural events or explain how the nearby towns came to be called as they are. You'll even find stretches of the Old Trace, sunken in over time due to the heavy wagon traffic it carried. As time permits, you'll want to stop and take in these different exhibits, especially the sunken trace.

THE ROUTE FROM TUPELO

0   Start on Hwy 278 at Natchez Trace South on-ramp

79.0   Turn left on SR 407 to Historic French Camp on left

67.0   Jeff Busby Site

79.1   Return on SR 407 to Parkway and turn left

151.0 Overlook on Ross Barnett Reservoir

171.0 Go west on Interstate 20

216.0 Continue to Vicksburg or take Parkway south to Natchez

You can slake your thirst and satisfy your hunger for history at the Council House Cafe just off the Natchez Trace Parkway in French Camp. The plastic folding tables are probably not authentic from the time period but are thankfully comfortable and stable.

If you need to top off your tank, stop at the only gas pump on the entire 444 mile route. At Mile 67 (Natchez Trace Milepost 193.1) is the **Jeff Busby Site** which has a convenience store and service station. The campground is named for **Thomas Jefferson Busby,** the U.S. Congressman from Mississippi, who introduced a bill that led to the Natchez Trace Parkway being added to the National Park System. You might not be able to tell by looking, but Jeff Busby Park is located on **Little Mountain** which is one of the highest points (elevation 603 feet) on the Parkway in Mississippi. The area includes an 18-site campground, picnic tables, and an exhibit shelter.

At Mile 79 (Natchez Trace Mile Marker 181) you'll come to French Camp (www.frenchcamp.org, 662-547-6835). Turn left on Hwy 413 for a couple hundred yards and turn left into the **French Camp Village.** The first building you'll come to is the **Huffman Cabin Gift Shop.** Construction began on the first room in 1840 a couple of miles south of French Camp by **George Marquess** and he finished the second room and a "dog trot" breezeway in 1852. In 1975 the cabin was relocated to its present location. The term "dog trot" (also "possum trot") refers to the breezeway between two separate cabins which was used as a simple method of ventilation for rural folk. Dogs would often lounge in the cool breezes generated by the shade of this connecting structure. It also became synonymous with poor people, as in "his family lived in an old dog trot house down by the creek and now he thinks he can socialize with us!"

If you arrive at the right time, sample a bit of Mississippi Mud Cake at the **Council House Cafe,** located in the rear of the gift shop cabin. The Council House was the meeting place for the last Chief of the Choctaw Indian Nation east of the Mississippi.

After a snack, you can walk or ride your bike through the historic district and see the **Col. James Drane House,** a 1900s-era post office, and a blacksmith shop. Stop in the Welcome Center with its bread bakery for the best loaf in Mississippi. If you're interested in staying over a couple of days and using this as your base, call ahead for reservations at the Drane House, the only bed-and-breakfast located directly on the Trace.

Return to the Natchez Trace heading south toward Jackson. In just under 70 miles the **Ross R. Barnett Reservoir,** fed by the **Pearl River,** will come into view. The reservoir overlook is a wonderful place to stop and enjoy a picnic lunch or just to stretch your legs and watch the boats on the water and wish you'd remembered to bring your swimming clothes.

Visitors are invited to wander through French Camp and the historic period dwelling at whatever pace best suits them. If you're looking for unique overnight accommodations check out the bed and breakfast located on site.

I like to keep a little snack in my saddlebags when I find places to take a break from the road, like this overlook at the Ross R. Barnett reservoir near Jackson, Mississippi.

When you're refreshed, return to the Trace and continue into **Jackson.** Depending on the progress of the construction on this section of the Parkway you may be dumped into Jackson proper. If the construction is finished, you can virtually bypass Jackson and reach the intersection with I-20 on the west side of town. If not, you'll have to take the detour. If that's the case, don't despair, just pick up Interstate 55 temporarily heading south, and then merge onto I-20 heading west. In a few miles you'll come to the section where the Parkway again intersects your route. It's at this juncture that you have the option of returning to the Parkway and heading south to Natchez, or continuing onto historic Vicksburg, where the history and charm of the Old South is inescapable. From the murals painted on the floodwall at the waterfront, to the grand mansions, the **Vicksburg National Military Park,** the fine bed-and-breakfast establishments and eateries, Vicksburg is rightly dubbed the **Red Carpet City of The South.**

Much of the history of Vicksburg can be seen in the 19 murals at the floodwall along its waterfront. One such mural depicts the famous presidential hunt where the term "teddy bear" was coined. On Nov. 14 1902, President **Theodore Roosevelt** was hunting 25 miles north of Vicksburg when his guide cornered a small 200-pound bear and tied the cub to a tree. The President refused to shoot the animal and a political cartoonist immortalized the scene.

Soon toy makers started producing "Teddy's Bears" which soon was shortened to teddy bears.

Before the teddy bear, there was the Civil War. Military strategists on both sides understood Vicksburg's strategic importance. Because of its height overlooking the Mississippi, the town became known as the **"Gibraltar of the Confederacy."** For forty-five days the inhabitants resisted the Union siege, living in caves dug into the hillside, until finally raising the white flag on July 3, 1863. The city officially surrendered the next day on July 4th and such was the insult to the pride of the town that Vicksburg did not celebrate the 4th of July for 81 years, until after World War II. To gain a better understanding of this epic struggle, visit the **Vicksburg National Military Park** (3201 Clay Street, www.nps.gov/vick, 601-636-0583). The park is open every day of the year except Christmas Day, from 8 a.m. to 5 p.m. Also in the Park is the **USS Cairo Gunboat and Museum.** The Cairo was sunk in the **Yazoo River** north of Vicksburg after striking underwater mines planted by the Confederates. The *Ironclad* was soon covered by the mud and silt of the river and sat undisturbed for 102 years to be raised in 1964, and later restored. Artifacts recovered from the ship provide a priceless snapshot into the daily lives of the soldiers and sailors during the War.

Regardless of which side you stand on in the Pepsi-Coke Wars, a visit to the **Biedenharn Candy Company Coca-Cola Museum** (1107 Washington Street) is worthy of your time. It was near this location in 1894 that **Joe Biedenharn** struck upon the idea to package Coca-Cola in bottles and distribute it to the rural area surrounding Vicksburg. Up to this time the only way to enjoy the popular soft drink was at a soda fountain where the syrup was mixed with water and served either over ice or straight up. Biedenharn and the executives at Coke soon realized the potential for bottled soda, as did thousands of imitators. But, Coke soon developed and patented its distinctive bottle, the first bottle patent issued at the time. Incidentally, the price for Coke then was just 78 cents a case! Admission to the museum is $3 for adults, $2 for children ages 6 to 12, and it is open Monday through Saturday 9 to 5 p.m. and on Sunday 1:30 to 4:30 p.m.

For the ultimate stay in a bed-and-breakfast, check out **Anchuca** (1010 First East Street, 601-661-0111). Anchuca means, "happy home," in Choctaw and you're sure to be happy after spending a night in the master suite here. The rates start at $210 per night, but remember it's Vicksburg oldest bed-and-breakfast and history does have its price.

If riverboat gambling suits your fancy then the **Horizon Casino Hotel** (1310 Mulberry Street, 601-636-3423), located directly on the riverfront, is your ticket. I've stayed here and can vouch for the rooms which start somewhere north of $80 per night.

Italian/Creole food is the specialty at **Borrellos** (1306 Washington Street, open 11 to 10 p.m. Monday through Sunday, 601-638-0169). Housed in a 1840s-era building, the huge wooden ceiling beams in the main dining area are meant to symbolize Noah's Ark. The fried pickles and fried eggplant appetizers are a must to try as well as Mama Borello's spaghetti and meatballs which currently is the Thursday special on the lunch menu.

Another local favorite is **Rusty's Riverfront Grill** (901 Washington Street, 601-638-2030). The food at Rusty's is well prepared and seasoned but if it's a busy night, you might have to wait awhile, and like any bustling restaurant, the place can be noisy. Speaking of local flavor, **Rowdy's Family Catfish Shack** (601-638-2375) at the intersection of Hwy 27 and Hwy 80 (Exit 5B off I-20) has been serving Mississippi pond-raised catfish just about any way you want 'em for the past 50 years. Fried, grilled, or blackened, and served with a side of batter fries and a dressing concoction, they'll simply knock your socks off! Rowdy's is open 10:45 to 9:30 p.m. Sunday through Thursday and 10:45 to 10 p.m. on Friday and Saturday.

Another fun Vicksburg attraction is **Yesterday's Children Antique Doll and Toy Museum** (1104 Washington Street, www.yesterdayschildrenmuseum.com). This might not seem much like a biker destination, but you might be surprised. While your sweetie is oohing and ahhing over the collection of

Because there isn't commercial development, traffic is light to moderate most times of the year, and you rarely have to contend with hordes of tourists seeking the latest and greatest mindless diversions. I seek the quiet secluded spots on the Natchez Trace Parkway.

At different spots along the route you can dismount and walk sections of the actual Trace which are preserved as they were when they were used in the 1700s. Think about how easy it would be for highway bandits to waylay travelers in areas such as this. (Photo by Sylvia Cochran)

dolls, you can browse the metal toy display from the 1920s to the 1980s. Trucks, cars, tractors, trains, motorcycles, planes, boats, soldiers, GI Joes, rocking horses, toy guns, and dump trucks and much more are all there. I hate to admit it but I used to play with many of these same type toys. Man, this place makes me feel dated!

And, if Antebellum homes are of interest, then you have to visit in early October for the annual **Pilgrimage of Homes** (www.vicksburgpilgrimage.com, 800-221-3536) which is coordinated by the **Vicksburg Convention and Visitors Bureau.** During this time you can tour these privately owned homes and experience a splendor period of our southern history.

When you're ready, I recommend heading back east on Clay Street to SR 27, turn right, and travel 16.5 miles to the Natchez Trace Parkway, and turn right again for the short 58 mile trip into **Natchez.**

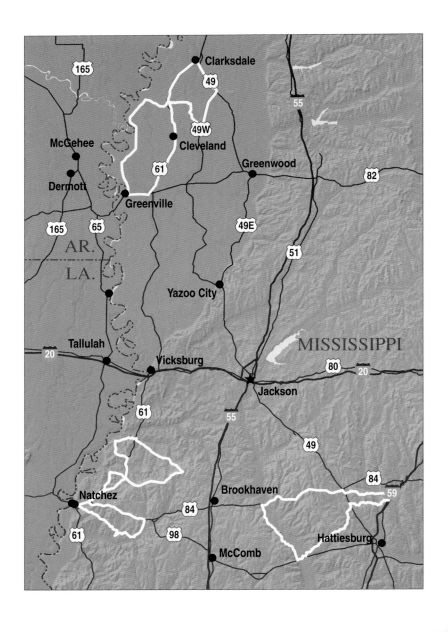

Bluffs, the Blues, & Lost Gold

Mississippi, a Jewel of Southern Charm

The Red Bluffs provide the local bikers with a destination and a reason to ride.

While Mississippi doesn't have much of the adrenaline pumping, peg scraping, twisty mountain roads which makes some of you live to ride, it has an abundance of small towns and cities that are unspoiled by the vulgarity we call progress in the 21st century. I say that with tongue-in-cheek because I often take advantage of the predictable sameness of the hotel and restaurant chains as I travel. However, there's nothing I enjoy more than visiting a region rich with history and cities that have remained virtually unchanged in the past 100 years.

Don't assume that you won't see a Super Wal-Mart in Vicksburg or Natchez. You'll also spot the Golden Arches on every corner in the large towns on the Great River. But more than any other state in the American South, I get the sense that Mississippi hasn't yet swept clean its dust bins of history or abandoned its sense of pride in the heritage of its Grand Past. In this section, I have endeavored to take you to the cities and the attractions which give the region its unique flavor and depth of spirit.

Of course, a travel book covering the American South wouldn't be complete without exploring the **Mississippi Delta.** As a population center, the Delta is young but its contribution to the popular culture in America looms larger than almost any other region in the South. It was home to notable figures such as **William Faulkner** and **Tennessee Williams.** The Delta is also where the legend of the "teddy bear" started after **Theodore Roosevelt** saved a bear cub from being shot on a Presidential hunting expedition. It is where a young boy from

Hot tamales and steak are the specialty at Doe's Eat Place in Greenville, Mississippi. (Photo by Amy Evans)

Tupelo developed his style of music and learned to swivel his hips eventually landing **Elvis Presley** on the national stage and crowning him the **King of Rock and Roll.**

The area was mostly swamp a century ago when cotton farming brought slaveholders and sharecroppers to settle the land. For the poor, life in the Delta was an endless struggle, and out of this desperation came the music we know as the **Blues.** It would be impossible to visit the Mississippi Delta and avoid the influence of the Blues. I can't say that I ever had much feel for the music before I spent some time in the area, but after the towns of **Rosedale, Clarksdale, Drew, Greenville, Greenwood,** and **Indianola,** were finished with me, I began searching out the music of **Son House, John Hooker, Charlie Patton, Muddy Waters, Howlin Wolf, Robert Johnson,** and **Mississippi John Hurt.**

The Blues has a way of infecting your soul with a sense that no matter how bad things are at the moment, you'll feel better just by singing about them. The term *The Blues* comes from the old Negro reference to "having a fit of the blue devils" which means being down in spirit, depressed, and sad. For me the music has a cleansing property much the same as the time I spend in the saddle of my motorcycle.

If singing the Blues leaves you a little sad, then there is the pick-me-up of authentic Delta comfort foods, Barbeque, Tamales, black eyed peas and ham hocks, green beans and cornbread and steaks. I wouldn't have included steak as an authentic Delta food were it not for a visit to **Doe's Eat Place** in Greenville. Doe's is legendary for its food and besides the tamales that every self respecting restaurant in the region serves, Doe's serves the best steaks for miles around. While we're on the topic of steak, the **Brandon House** in Columbia has sirloin steak for $10! Anytime the doors are open, the steak meal is $10, including sides and drink. The buffet style lunch and casual dinner attracts the locals like bees to honey so come early! Fish lovers will want to call ahead to the **Old Watermill Catfish Camp** (195 Old Watermill Road, Ellisville, 601-752-2395). I can't personally vouch for the food but I have acquaintances who swear by it.

The best fried chicken I've tasted in a very long time was in **Lorman** on a Sunday at the **Old Country Store** (18801 US 61, 601-437-3661, 10 to 6 p.m. daily). The Old Country Store is just as its name implies and the 130 year old wooden structure is showing her age. Back in its day, the building provided farmers and settlers with all the necessities of country living. From work boots to caskets, this store was where you'd purchase the simple necessities of rural living, if you couldn't make them yourself. Today, Authur Davis works his culinary wizardry on that staple of the southern diet, fried chicken. He also whips up a mean batch of cornbread. If you act right, he'll come to your table and sing about his Grandmamma, the "Cornbread cooking queen."

Located on the road less traveled, the Ruins of Windsor are the perfect setting for a romance novel or murder mystery.

For more mouthwatering home cooking, you have to stop in at **People's Choice Restaurant** in **Drew,** the hometown of football legend **Archie Manning.** Besides serving tasty food, the owners treat you like home folks and will sit and talk to you a spell, if they're not busy serving the hungry lunch crowd.

In **Clarksdale,** you'll find local pork flavor at **Abe's BBQ** (616 North State Street, Clarksdale, 662-624-9947). If you're famished, try the double decker "Big Abe" which is served overflowing with pork meat and slaw on a flimsy paper plate! Abe's is a stone's throw from the legendary **Crossroads of the Blues,** US 64 and US 49. For more on this legend and controversy see Trip 17: Singing the Blues in Clarksdale on page 184. But don't fill up on barbeque because you'll want to save room for a **fried tomato sammich!** I know, that's not the way Webster spells it but you need to read the chapter to fully appreciate it.

For accommodations, Mississippi has a wide range of choices. From the **Horizon Casino Riverboat** in Vicksburg (www.horizonvicksburg.com) or the numerous antebellum homes in Natchez (www.natchezpilgrimage.com) to the B&B (Bed and Beer) sharecropper shack rental at the **Shack Up Inn** located on the Hopson Plantation just outside of Clarksdale (rates from $50 to $75 per night), there's something for everyone. In **Clarksdale** you can sleep, or try to sleep above an authentic operating southern juke joint. **Ground Zero** (www.groundzerobluesclub.com), which is owned by the movie star **Morgan Freeman** has rates which start at $75 per night and go up from there. The rooms have names such as "Good Middling," "Low Middling," and "Strict Low Middling," designating different grades of cotton. After all, this is the South and the building used to be home to the Delta Cotton Company where keen eyed graders would judge the quality of cotton by holding it up to the light coming in from the skylight. Remember this is a working juke joint so don't expect a lot of peace and quiet while the joint's jumpin!

We'll also ride over near **Columbia** to a little known local attraction provided by Mother Nature. The Red Bluff run is what happens when rain water and soft red clay meet and rainwater wins. It just so happens that this attraction is conveniently located on a nice two-lane twisty section of highway that would be fun to ride for no other reason than the road itself.

Sometimes the destination is the reason for the ride and in **Port Gibson** the destination is the **Ruins of Windsor.** The first time I visited the area I was looking at a map for squiggly lines and found Rodney Road. Then a local told me about the Ruins of Windsor located on that road. What luck! Someone took a great motorcycle road and put a neat historical attraction near the end of it. How thoughtful! If the word "Windsor" brings to mind a castle, then you're close.

And since we're wasting time, let's start riding and get there!

Trip 17   Singing the Blues in Clarksdale

Distance   *180 miles*
Terrain   *Flat asphalt. Rough patches in places, potholes in others. Traffic light in the country, moderate in the towns.*
Highlights   *The Great Wall of Mississippi, Native American mounds, Crossroads of the Blues, sharecropper cabin accommodations, an authentic Delta juke joint*

We'll start this journey in **Greenville,** Mississippi. Greenville is known for having more published writers per capita than any other city in the U.S. The town was founded in 1828 on the banks of the great river that refuses to be tamed. Ever since man inhabited the region around this waterway, the **Mississippi River** has nurtured and alternately ruined the lives of those living along its floodplains and Greenville has seen its share of those ups and downs. The Great Flood of 1927 is still remembered and its impact is felt today. There are several museums in the downtown area that tell the story of that flood and the

While Rosedale residents dispute it, the generally accepted Crossroads of the Blues is in Clarksdale, Mississippi, where highways 49 and 61 intersect.

reconstruction of the levee. Before you leave town you must ride to the waterfront and atop what is now called the **Great Wall of Mississippi** (www.thedelta.org, 662-334-2711). After the mighty river broke through the levee just north of town, it was rebuilt and now exceeds the length of the Great Wall of China!

For barbeque lovers, the locals all recommend the **Shotgun House** (223 Central Street, Greenville, 662-334-9685). But probably the most famous restaurant in the area is **Doe's Eat Place** (502 Nelson Street, 662-334-3315). Doe's is family owned and operated and while it's not much to look at, the food is both Italian and genuine Mississippi Delta like no other outside the region. The son of an Italian immigrant, Doe Signa began selling tamales to the neighborhood's black customers in 1941 from a juke joint at the front of the family home. White customers began to visit the rear of the house for steaks, spaghetti, and tamales to go. Over time the restaurant took over the juke joint and Doe's Eat House was born. Now, on a typical day Doe's will serve 50 dozen tamales and over 80 steaks. You don't want to miss this one.

THE ROUTE FROM GREENVILLE

0   US 82 at SR 1

45.8   Right on SR 32

56.5   Left on North Broad Street

56.5   Right on East School Avenue

56.6   Cross four lane 278/61

65.9   Turn right on Lombardy Drive when pavement ends

78.1   Right on North Main Street

78.2   Right on Wilson Avenue to US 49W/SR 3

78.5   Left on US 49 West

93.0   Merge with US 49 East and continue north

106.0 Left onto Hopson Road to Shack Up Inn

106.5 Left back onto US 49

109.5 At intersection of US 49 and 61, turn left on 61

109.8 Right on Sunflower Avenue

110.6 Right on 3rd Street

110.8 Right on Delta Avenue to Ground Zero Blues Club

174.7 Take US 61 south to US 82 and turn right

179.8 Arrive back in Greenville, Mississippi

Reset your odometer at the intersection of US 82 and SR 1 and head north on SR 1. The first thing you'll notice is how flat the terrain seems. It seems that way because it is! On this journey you won't have much opportunity to practice nailing the apex because the residents you meet adopt the laid back, almost lazy pace of the nearby river. At Mile 6, you'll reach **Winterville Mounds State Park** on your right. The grounds are open daily from dawn to dusk and the museum is open 9 to 5 Monday through Saturday and 1:30 to 5 p.m. on Sunday. Admission is free. The mounds were built by a Native American civilization that thrived from 1000 to 1400 A.D. Even though you just got started, this is a good place to stop and learn about the history of the Native American tribes along the Great River.

Leave Winterville Mounds and continue north on SR 1 toward the town of **Rosedale**. At Mile 35.1, you'll come to the intersection of SR 1 and SR 8 and you'll need to watch for the Devil's X in the middle of the road.

Okay, actually there's no X in the road, but the legend of the Devil's X can be traced to a relatively unknown bluesman by the name of **Robert Johnson.**

As a blues player it was said that Johnson had no contemporary equal. His song, *Crossroads,* has been covered by **Eric Clapton,** and his music has influenced artists such as the **Rolling Stones, Led Zeppelin,** and the **Red Hot Chili Peppers.** In his song *Crossroads,* Johnson doesn't give any clues as to which town may rightfully claim the crossroads of the blues but he does say he fell down on his knees, asking the Lord for forgiveness, perhaps for his deal with the devil?

As you might guess, the location of the legendary crossroads is hotly disputed in the Delta. Lots of towns in central Mississippi claim to be the crossroads of musical lore with the two leading candidates being Rosedale and Clarksdale. The intersection you've reached at Mile 35.2 is the one that some Rosedale residents say was the actual location of the legend. But, Clarksdale, where Highways 61 and 48 converge is the spot that is generally accepted as the crossroads in the myth.

Other Rosedale residents counter that it couldn't be because everyone knows that the Devil sticks close to the Mississippi!

This spot marks the crossroads of controversy in Rosedale, Mississippi, where some locals claim Robert Johnson made his deal with the devil. Others claim it was in nearby Clarksdale.

Continue on SR 1 north and at Mile 45.8, turn right on SR 32 and head to the town of Shelby. Continue on SR 32 through Shelby, and at Mile 56.5, SR 32 deadends into North Broad Street. Turn left and immediately back right on East School Avenue. In a couple thousand feet you'll come to 278/61. Use caution crossing this busy four lane highway. Continue across on SR 32 and nine miles later the pavement ends at Lombardy Drive where you turn right. The next 12 miles will take you past fields and farms that make up part of the vast agricultural network of the Delta. While the elevation doesn't change, this section of our journey has enough twists and turns to keep you from falling asleep. At Mile 77, you'll enter **Drew,** the boyhood home of civil rights leader **Mae Bertha Carter** and of football legend **Archie Manning.** At Mile 78.1, turn right on North Main Street and if you're hungry, visit **People's Choice Restaurant** (125 North Main Street, Drew, 662-745-0193). In my humble opinion, Walter and Jessie Scularks serve the best homemade $6 lunch anywhere in the

The Legend of the Devil's X

Robert Johnson was something of a ne'er do well and like many bluesmen in his day, he lived hand-to-mouth, playing Delta juke joints for food or the money taken in at the door when he performed. It is said that Johnson once was told by Son House, another famous bluesman, to put away that guitar because his style made people nervous and ran off customers. Supposedly Johnson wasn't seen for a while around his usual haunts and a few months later when he returned to the Blues scene, he could play a guitar like no one else alive. Rumors started flying that Johnson had sold his soul to the devil. Someone, perhaps Johnson himself, began telling of his encounter with the Devil. According to Delta legend, when the moon is full, the Devil will come to the Delta, and place his X in the middle of a deserted crossroad, hoping to snare a bluesman, because musicians, especially blues players it is said, will do anything to be the best guitar player alive, even if it means pledging their soul to the Devil. It was at such a crossroads on a cool October night that Johnson met a sharply dressed stranger who offered Johnson the gift. The Devil asked Johnson, "You want to be the King of the Delta Blues and have all the whiskey and women you want?" "Yea, devil-man, I gots to have dem blues" said Johnson. So the deal was struck and Johnson was on his way to becoming a legend in the Delta. But alas, the Devil also took his due and Johnson died young and penniless. ■

This mural is painted on the side of Gilbow's drug store in Drew, Mississippi, which incidentally is the birthplace of football legend Archie Manning, father to Eli and Peyton Manning.

Delta, so you won't want to miss this bargain. When you're finished, head down the street to **Gilbow's Drug Store** (103 North Main Street) for authentic old Drug Store charm. As you leave town, turn right on Wilson Avenue and travel a couple of blocks to the **Little Red Schoolhouse** on your left. This school was one of over 5,000 constructed in the South for black children before desegregation by the Rosenwald Fund which was started in the early 1900s by the CEO of Sears, Roebucks & Co, Julius Rosenwald. Out of 633 Rosenwald buildings built in the 1900s, only eleven now remain.

Turn left on US 49W/SR 3 at Mile 78.5, and at Mile 93, you'll merge left with US 49E and continue north. At Mile 106, turn left onto Hopson Road, and across the railroad track, you'll enter a time machine set to carry you back to the 1970s, the **Shack Up Inn** (001 Commissary Circle, Clarksdale, www.shackupinn.com, 662-624-8329). Up until a few years ago, Hopson Plantation was an active agricultural operation but in 1998 it was de-commissioned so to speak and today serves as a most unusual tourist B&B. Here, that stands for bed and beer, not bed and breakfast. Bill Talbot and James Butler rescued a few of the original shotgun sharecropper shacks on the plantation, and renovated them. Well, renovated might be a bit overstated but they did install a window air-conditioner, a gas heater for the winter, and indoor

The brochure says it's Mississippi's oldest B & B, (bed and beer) and they might be right. If you're tired of the same old thing from the hotel chains, then spend a night at the Shack Up Inn in Hopson and you'll have something to tell your friends!

plumbing, but that's about it. Each shack has a front porch which allowed the original owners to view the world as it passed by and a place to socialize with friends and neighbors. I'd also imagine a few old dogs slept their summers away under these porches. The shacks are what serve as overnight accommodations for visitors seeking a genuine Delta Blue experience. Don't expect matching sheets and pillow cases, and don't look for anything wider than a double bed, but they are clean and well maintained. If you're a big guy and need something more, the owners have made a few more rooms from the grain bins inside the cotton gin. The beds are queen sized in those. On weekends, the old Commissary at the Inn hosts local blues musicians, some famous, most not, but all talented. Rates start at $50 and go up to $75. It's an unusual overnight stop you don't want to miss.

Continuing north on US 49 to Clarksdale, you'll pass under US 61 bypass but continue straight. At Mile 109.5, you'll arrive at the intersection of US 49 and 61 and **Abe's Famous BBQ**, located a few feet from the famous Blues Crossroads of Highways 61 and 48. Abe's is known both statewide and as far away as California as the best barbeque in the Delta.

This junction is internationally recognized as the **"Crossroads of the Blues."** Clarksdale does a better job than any other town in promoting itself as Ground Zero for the Blues movement. But, the town has had some help from Hollywood actor **Morgan Freeman,** the star of *Drivin Miss Daisy, The Shawshank Redemption,* and my personal favorite, *Unforgiven* with Clint Eastwood. Turn left on US 61 and travel 3/10 of a mile and turn right on Sunflower Avenue. At 110.6, turn right on 3rd Street and take the next right on

Delta Avenue. A hundred yards or so on your right is where Freeman, a blues afficionado, and a couple of local businessmen, bought what can only be described as an authentic Delta juke joint. I can promise you **Ground Zero** (www.groundzerobluesclub.com), isn't a Hollywood recreation because I grew up around juke joints and while my parents didn't know and certainly wouldn't have approved, I spent many a summer day in my hometown of Keysville, Georgia, hanging out in a juke called **The Brown Derby.** It's where I learned to play pool and recognize a bar fight long before it breaks out, so I can spot authentic and this one is the real deal. The first thing you notice when you pull up to the front of Ground Zero is the eclectic mix of furniture that could have been salvaged from the local landfill. Wasting time at Ground Zero is done the same way it's been done for decades at juke joints across the South. It's easy to imagine the origin of the rips in the vinyl as coming from an errant swipe of a switchblade and the stains on the flattened cushions as the result of an excessive night of drinking. Forget about being squeamish. Just be sure to bring your own Sharpie, the pen, that is, because everyone who visits here finds a bare spot to sign their name. Over the years, thousands of names have been added to every square inch of Ground Zero. The pool tables, lights, tables, chairs, bar, and barstools are covered in signatures. While I was there the waitress made the mistake of standing still for longer than a minute and someone signed her arm!

Actor Morgan Freeman says this is his favorite Mississippi juke joint, and you can believe that because he owns it! It's not much to look at from the outside but don't let that stop you from a visit.

If it's slow, and the joint's not jumping, the staff have been known to allow a biker to bring his motorcycle inside for a picture in front of the stage, although that favor requires quite a bit of sweet talking and a pretty big tip. If you arrive here at lunchtime, or anytime you're good and hungry, you have to try the fried green tomato *sammich*. Yes, that's spelled right, it's sammich, not sandwich. Made with fried green tomatoes, Monterey Jack and Mozzarella cheese, topped with bacon, smothered in GZ Gitback sauce, and served on a dirty white bun, I can honestly say I've never tasted better. There's also a "BBQ sundae" that's made with layers of pulled smoked pork shoulder, barbeque beans, and cole slaw that tastes as good as it sounds.

If you're really adventurous, spend the night *over* Ground Zero in the **Delta Cotton Company Apartments** (662-645-9366). Prices start at $75 per night and go up from there, but stay seven days or longer and you'll get a discount! Remember these rooms are *over* the juke joint, so don't plan on snoozing when the band is bluezin! (I made that last word up!)

Across the way from Ground Zero is the **Delta Blues Museum** (1 Blues Alley, Clarksdale, 662-627-6820), a must see for students of the Blues Admission is adults $7, children $5 (under age 6 free), and the museum is open March

Juke Joints

The term *juke joint* is sometimes incorrectly used instead of *honky tonk*. For the most part, a juke joint is a black establishment, while a honky tonk is a white establishment. The origin of the word "juke" is unknown. Some think it comes from the jukebox that was frequently found in these establishments or it may originate from the Gullah word joog meaning "rowdy or disorderly."

In larger communities, juke joints were located primarily in the African-American sections of town and rarely if ever had white patrons. In rural areas, the distinction was based more on wealth and society status than race, but the owners of the juke joints were usually African Americans. Often the buildings were nothing more than old houses converted for the purpose of serving bootleg alcohol and providing a place for the patrons to gamble or dance to local blues musicians. With the abundance of alcohol, the presence of women of questionable repute, and the rough and tumble lifestyle of the patrons, frequent fights erupted resulting in a shooting or a razor cutting. Today juke joints have been replaced by hip hop clubs and the jazz music often by rap. ∎

Known as the Great Wall of Mississippi, this levee is longer than the Great Wall of China and is partially paved for a stretch so you can ride on its top for several miles at a stretch. (Photo by Sylvia Cochran)

through October, 9 to 5 p.m. on Monday through Saturday and November through February, 10 to 5 p.m. and on Monday through Saturday.

The Mississippi Delta is known throughout the world as the Birthplace of the Blues and the most famous entertainer to be influenced by this culture was Elvis Presley. When the King of Rock and Roll moved from his boyhood home of Tupelo, Mississippi, to Memphis, Tennessee, he moved directly into the path of Hwy 61. Hwy 61 is etched into Blues lore because it was the main road used to travel north from the Delta out of poverty to the promise of a new life in the northern towns of Chicago and St. Louis. But Elvis, as famous as he was, did not truly shape blues music. Instead, it was men such as Muddy Waters, W.C. Handy, John Lee Hooker, Elmore James, Riley B. King a/k/a B.B. King, and the souls of hundreds of other men and women who walked the crossroads and told their stories of life, love, and living in the Mississippi Delta.

To return to Greenville, take Hwy 61 south to where it intersects with US 82 in **Leland** and turn right.

Trip 18   Mississippi Red Bluff

Distance   *145.3 miles*

Terrain   *Flat, two-lane road with a few curvy sections. Asphalt is good in sections, poor in others. Use caution and watch for pea gravel. Traffic is light in the country, moderate in town.*

Highlights   *Twisty two lane roads, Bluff overlook, recreated 50s drug store, old time grist mill*

Begin this ride where Interstate 59 meets Hwy 29 near the town of **Ellisville,** Mississippi, at exit 88. Head north for .8 miles and turn left on SR 588. Shortly you'll come upon a historical roadside plaque commemorating the **Skirmish At Rocky Creek,** where a 40 man Union force was "defeated" by the local Confederates. If you're a visitor to the American South, there is one thing you'll soon discover. We're proud of our rebellious heritage. Without getting into a long tirade about the War of Northern Aggression, I can tell you that almost every town and county in the Deep South has historical markers similar to this one in little out of the way places. Erected not to glorify the horrors of war, but to remind us that our forefathers fought a gallant fight for their homelands. Despite the misrepresentation of their motives, we're proud of them and yes, even after all these years, we're still a touch defiant.

Mother Nature finally reclaimed the land under Mississippi State Route 587 and traffic has been diverted some 300 yards away. In a few years, even this asphalt will crumble.

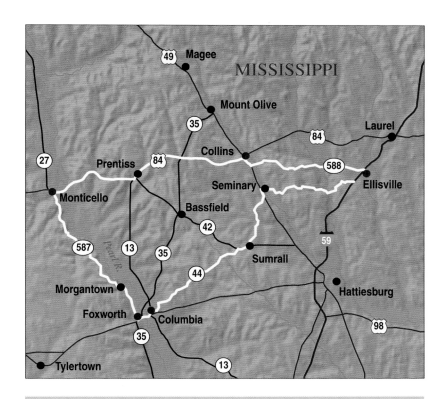

THE ROUTE FROM ELLISVILLE

0   Hwy SR 588 at SR 29
21.5   Left on SR 84
41.6   Turn left to stay on 84
59.0   Turn left onto SR 587
88.7   Turn left onto SR 35/US 98
94.0   Turn left on SR 44
113.0 Turn right on SR 42
115.0 Turn left on SR 589 (Main Street)
126.3 Turn left on US 49
126.4 Turn right on SR 590
137.0 Turn right on Old Watermill Road (turn around)
138.0 Turn right on SR 590
145.0 End at I-59

Central Mississippi residents love to use "pea gravel" in driveways and dirt road entrances, which ranks right up there on my list with deer and armadillo as least favorite things to encounter while riding my motorcycle. (Photo by Sylvia Cochran)

21.4 miles later turn left on Hwy 84 heading through the town of **Collins.** Collins retains much of its traditional past. Keeping in mind that the journey is more important than the destination, I'd recommend stopping and taking a stroll down Main Street. Sit on one of the park benches and soak up small town charm. It's disappearing from the South at a rate much faster than I like to admit.

You'll leave Collins heading west still on Hwy 84. At 41.6 miles, you'll turn left to stay on Hwy 84 as you approach the **Pearl River** and the town of **Monticello.** There is a campground on the Pearl River and if you're in the mood to relax, drop your kickstand and enjoy the hospitality of the local riders.

Turn left on SR 587 a/k/a Robinwood Road, and head south. I have ridden a fair amount of central Mississippi and SR 587 is a highway with good news and bad news. The good news is that for the next 20 some miles there are enough curves to keep even the most aggressive sports riders content, but the bad news is that the asphalt road hasn't been maintained very well and you are forced to ride too slow to entertain any thoughts of draggin' a knee or scrubbing your pipes.

I keep hoping MDOT (Mississippi Department of Transportation) will hire a motorcycle enthusiast as their Director and he or she will see that this could become the best stretch of motorcycle highway within a couple hundred mile radius and lobby for the funds to resurface the road.

This is as good a point as any to talk about another quaint custom in central Mississippi and that is the use of a product called "pea gravel." Named because it resembles those bright green canned peas that look delicious. The locals use it to line their driveways as erosion control. Inevitably some of it will wash into the road during a spring or summer frog strangler (that's a heavy rain for you "non-Southerners"). Riding over a short patch of these ball bearing sized rocks in a sharp curve while executing a hero lean will result in a case of low side black-and-blues.

That being said, I included this road in the book for a couple of reasons. The first being that twisty roads in central Mississippi are about as easy to find as June bugs in August, and second there is a little known natural landmark that you must detour long enough to see.

To enjoy a malt the way it used to be, stop at Cranford's Drug Store in Sumrall, Mississippi.

Local enthusiasts call this Red Bluff Road, and around 85 miles after starting this journey you'll come upon the landmark. Set high on a hill overlooking the Pearl River Valley is a large washed out section of red clay hillside known as the Red Bluff. In years past, each time the approaching erosion threatened to undercut the asphalt MDOT highway planners shifted the road several feet away. On a recent trip, MDOT had surrendered the road 300 yards west to eliminate the cat-and-mouse game with Mother Nature. By the time this book is printed, the highway that runs by the Red Bluff will be closed to through traffic, although you should still be able to ride your bike to the edge of the bluff. You just won't be able to cross it, as the roadbed will soon collapse when the ground beneath is completely eroded away.

Standing on the bluff without the benefit of restraining walls or safety fences connects you to Mother Nature in a raw untamed way that makes this area attractive to motorcycle riders. You know that one slip and you will plunge 40 feet into the ravine below, quite possibly with fatal results. But to us, death is an old friend, and one we're comfortable with, so we stand and gaze 20 miles at the horizon and inhale the scent of the towering magnolia blooms on the trees below our feet and realize that it's good to be alive and riding a motorcycle in the American South.

Watermills like this one in Central Mississippi provided energy to grind corn into meal, grits, and flour. Today they're slowly vanishing from the landscape.

As you leave, you'll continue south on SR 587 until you reach **Foxworth** (not the home of **Jeff Foxworthy,** a great southern comedian) where you'll turn left on SR 35/US 98 and head into the town of **Columbia.**

At 91.6 miles, you'll turn left onto SR 13 or Lumberton Road and head into the town proper. This street will soon change names and become South High School Avenue. At 93 miles, you'll turn right on Broad Street, SR 198. You'll soon reach the driveway of the **Brandon House.** For buffet style lunch or casual dinner dining, the Brandon House is a local favorite. There is a seafood buffet Friday and Saturday nights. My favorite is the $10 sirloin, which is available anytime. It's hard to believe, but really, any time the doors are open the price is $10 and it includes your side and drink. That's a true southern deal.

At 94 miles, you'll turn left onto SR 44, a two lane, easy-winding country road that carries you into the town of **Sumrall.** If you've skipped all the other restaurants, the **Catfish Wagon** is located at the intersection of SR 44 and SR 42.

At Mile 113, turn right on SR 42 for two miles and then turn left on SR 589. At Mile 126.3, turn left on US 49 and .1 mile later turn back right on SR 590 into the town of **Seminary.** Once you get into town, pause at **Cranford's** for a malt in this (replicated) early Americana drug store. A few feet away is **Heather's Dixie Grill.** Anything named "Dixie" is worth taking a chance on, but I haven't sampled the fare so don't blame me if it's not up to your expectations. I'm sure the tea is cold and syrupy sweet, because that's a tradition in the South, and I'd bet they serve fried chicken (another southern delicacy), but that's just a guess.

At Mile 137, you can detour a short distance by turning right on Old Watermill Road for a little over a half a mile where you'll come to **Snow's Creek** and an authentic water grist mill right beside the road. It's a must do photo op, but beware that there isn't much of a shoulder for parking. While you might not encounter another vehicle during your stop, if you do, there isn't much room to escape unless you jump into the nearby creek.

The **Old Watermill CatFish Camp** (195 Old Watermill Road, Ellisville, 601-752-2395) stands ready to serve you fish, shrimp, and steaks Tuesday through Saturday. Unfortunately, my trips have always occurred on a Sunday or a Monday so I can't make any recommendation, but my experience tells me that any restaurant this far from a population center has to be good in order to stay in business.

This journey ends at Mile 149, the intersection of I-59 and CR 590.

Trip 19   Hunting the Roxie Hole Gold

Distance   *76 miles*

Terrain   *Sweeping curves on well-maintained asphalt with slight elevation changes. Watch for wildlife; not recommended for nighttime riding.*

Highlights   *Twisty roads through a national park, legends of lost gold, the devils punchbowl, a restored 1800s college, and a haunted tavern*

We'll begin and end this journey in the historic town of **Natchez**, Mississippi. The first Europeans to settle the area were the French in 1716 who founded **Fort Rosalie**, but the native tribes resented the new French settlers. Encouraged by British agents, the Natchez Indians resisted the French until war erupted and the French completely wiped out the entire Indian population. What remained of the Natchez people dispersed to other tribes, and eventually Fort Rosalie came under American control and was renamed Natchez after the extinguished tribe. For more of their history, you can visit the 128 acre site of the **Grand Village of the Natchez Indians** (400 Jefferson Davis Boulevard, 601-446-6502).

I didn't believe in the legend of the Roxy Hole gold until a local pointed me to this road, and well, the sign confirms it. Bring your own shovel and winch.

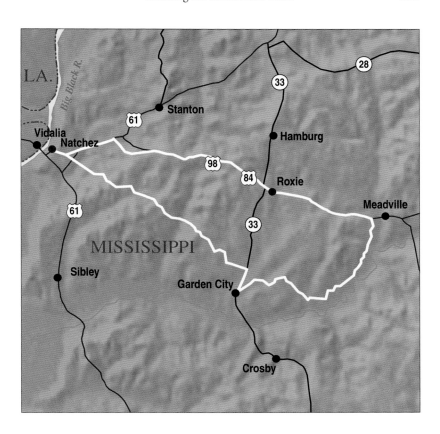

THE ROUTE FROM NATCHEZ

0   Franklin Street and North Canal Street
1.3   Right on Liberty Road
22.5   Right on SR 33
24.1   Left on Knoxville/Bunkley Road
43.5   Left on US 84/98
68.7   Right on US 64 to Jefferson College entrance
69.0   Entrance to college. Return to US 64 and turn right
76.0   End of journey at North Canal Street

In the keel and steamboat days, Natchez was divided into two distinct societies. Genteel and proper Southerners kept to themselves on the hill and bluffs overlooking the Mississippi River. Working class folks and boatmen who brought goods to the port in Natchez frequented the riverfront area known as Natchez Under the Hill. Even Mark Twain wrote about it in his *Life on the Mississippi* and described them as "coarse frolickers…every one, elephantinely jolly, foul-witted, profane; prodigal of their money, fond of barbaric finery, prodigious braggarts; yet, in the main, honest, trustworthy, faithful to promises and duty, and often picturesquely magnanimous." They sound like the sort of crowd I ride with at times!

For a slice of life on the Mississippi waterfront, try the Mark Twain Guest House located beside Natchez Under-The-Hill Saloon right on the river.

In June the town of Natchez reenacts the famous steamship race between the Robert E. Lee and the Natchez with Steamboat Jubilee & Floozy Day.

Today the hard drinking boatmen are extinct, having been replaced by tourists and businessmen. For a taste of what the area must have been like during its heyday, you can visit the **Under-The-Hill-Saloon** (25 Silver Street, 601-446-8023), or stay at the **Mark Twain Guest House** next door. There's no evidence that Twain really slept here, but I can promise you won't soon forget your time at the **Under-The-Hill Saloon** or its bartender, J.D.

If you time your arrival for the last weekend in June, you just might catch the reenactment of the annual **Natchez Steamboat Race** and Floozy Day. The original race was held in June 1870 between the boats *Robert E. Lee* and the *Natchez,* with the *Lee* setting a record time from New Orleans to St. Louis that still stands today for steamboats. Mark Twain said of steamboat racing, "this is a sport that makes a body's very liver curl with enjoyment." Hey, I'm all for curling my liver every now and again.

Down the street, the **Magnolia Grill** (49 Silver Street, 601-446-7670) is a little pricey for the economy-minded traveler but it has a nice view of the river from a glass enclosed dining area. A little further north, **The Cock of The Walk** (200 North Broadway, 601-446-8920) features a "boatman" theme decor and food. Before you rap me about this restaurant being an obvious tourist trap, you should know that their fried catfish is a favorite of the locals and the aluminum pie pan plates and tin cup drinkware sets this place apart from the "national chain" type restaurants.

When you've had your fill of food, head north on US 61 Bus (East Franklin Street). In two miles, you'll need to continue on Liberty Street as 61B merges with US 84 and 98. For the next 22 miles, Liberty Road carries you through the rolling hills of the **Homochitto National Forest.** Twisty and tight are the words to describe this stretch of highway. At Mile 22.5, turn right on SR 33 for 1.7 miles and then turn left on Bunkley/Knoxville Road. Bunkley also twists and turns through Homochitto and about 18 miles later you'll emerge at Mile 43.5 and US 84/98. Turn left.

In nine miles, you'll arrive in the town of **Roxie,** home to what some call a huge hoax and others call a legitimate lost gold legend. With less than 600 people, the locals don't talk much about the legend, or at least they didn't talk much to me. At **Woody's Diner** (129 West Street) the waitress just stared at me when I asked about the legend. I recognized that stare because I get it at Mexican restaurants when I ask for a double whopper with cheese. But there was an old timer sitting nearby who scribbled something on a napkin, laid it on my table, and walked away. It was a simple map, easy to follow, but there was also a warning which said, "you don't really want to go there!" But I did, so at the edge of town, I turned right on SR 33 and in 1.5 miles came to a dirt road on the left called Gold Hole Road! Maybe this was what that old man meant by his note. He was right—I really didn't want to travel down an unfamiliar dirt road!

So, I backtracked to SR 33 and US 64 and found someone at the convenience store who told me of an article in the *Brookhaven MS Daily Leader* about the legend. It seems that a gang of train robbers in the 1800s buried their loot in a sugar cane cauldron to hide it from the law during their getaway, intending to return and dig it up later. All but one was caught and the map was passed from person-to-person through the ensuing years. But, no one ever found the gold. One person claims to have gotten close, but each time he would latch onto what he believed was the cauldron, it would slip from the rope or cable and sink deeper into the hole. Since you're on a motorcycle with no way to tote a cauldron full of gold bars and coins, it's probably better you don't waste your time riding down Mississippi red clay dirt roads in search of it!

At Mile 68.7, where US 84/98 merges with US 64, you'll come to what the locals refer to as the **Devils Punchbowl,** an odd shaped depression that some say is haunted, although I didn't feel any spirits. Turn right for .5 miles to the entrance of historic **Jefferson College.** Open Monday through Friday 9 to 5 p.m., and Sunday 1 to 5 p.m., the college is preserved as a living 1800s museum and listed on the **National Register of Historic Places.** First opened in 1811, it was closed at the outbreak of the Civil War in 1863 and reopened in 1866 as a preparatory school, but was closed permanently as a learning institution in 1964. You can tour a restored dormitory room, student dining room,

Jefferson College is preserved as a living 1800s museum. First opened in 1811, it was closed at the outbreak of the Civil War in 1863.

kitchen buildings, and other historic sites. If the grounds look familiar to you it's because it was used as the scene of West Point Academy in the *North and the South* television mini-series, and in the movies *Horse Soldiers, Mistress of Paradise,* and two versions of *Huckleberry Finn.*

When you're finished touring the college return to US 61 and turn right. Leave and continue on US 61 84/98 west until you return to your starting point at Natchez-Under-The-Hill at Mile 75.5.

If touring antebellum homes strikes your fancy, then plan to arrive in spring or fall for the semi-annual **Natchez Pilgrimage.** Natchez was spared the torch that burned many of the cities in the South during the Civil War and today has over 500 surviving buildings that pre-date the 1860s. In fact, the tradition of the Grand Pilgrimage started in Natchez in the early 1930s when a freeze wiped out the blooms prior to a weekend garden tour. With tourists coming in from all over the region, the dames of Natchez were distraught. The suggestion was made to open the houses to the visiting tourists. Several of the prominent ladies were hesitant because their houses had not been renovated since the Civil War as money was tight during reconstruction. Despite their reservations, the tour was conducted and was a huge success. The biggest reason for its success it seems was precisely because the houses had not been changed much in the 60 years following the War. That's what visitors wanted to see then, and continues to lure tourists twice a year for the Pilgrimage.

According to local lore, the ghosts of several recently discovered skeletons haunt the Kings Tavern, the oldest building in Natchez.

If you have time to tour only one house in Natchez, then I strongly suggest you choose to visit **Longwood** (140 Lower Woodville Road, 601-442-5193). Dubbed **"Nutts Folly"** by the locals, Longwood is a romantic southern-era time capsule from the 1800s. Construction was begun in 1859 by **Dr. Haller Nutt,** a wealthy eastern cotton planter. The six floor Oriental style dwelling is the largest octagonal shaped house in America. Only the basement is completed, because at the outbreak of the Civil War the northern workmen abandoned their tools and boarded steamships back home to avoid being stranded during the blockades of the southern ports. Many of their tools lay scattered where they left them.

Even on the hottest day of the year you can stand on the balcony and feel the cool breeze wafting in from the large shaded area provided by the huge oak in the rear of the house. Even unfinished, the grandeur of the project awes the visitor. Dr. Nutt wasn't able to complete his "folly" because of the irony of war. Nutt remained loyal to the Union yet lost his cotton fortune when the blockade prevented his harvest from reaching market. Eventually his land was confiscated and remaining crops burned by Union soldiers. Nutt died of pneumonia in 1864, a financially ruined and emotionally broken man.

Unfulfilled grandeur is on display at Longwood. Begun by a wealthy cotton planter, the Civil War interrupted its construction and later caused the destruction of the fortune of its owner, thereby ensuring that it would never be completed. It's a must see if you love antebellum architecture. (Photo by Sylvia Cochran)

Built to attract passing tourists to her delicious food, this 28 foot tall Mammy has been serving patrons in her restaurant since the 1940s.

Tickets for the **Natchez Pilgrimage Tour** are sold by the day ($8 per house or $28 per person for a 4 house tour) and are available online at www.natchezpilgrimage.com or 1-800-647-6742. Some houses such as Longwood are available to tour year 'round.

By now all this hunting for lost treasure, touring antebellum homes, and visiting restored college campuses is sure to have made you hungry. Visit **Biscuits and Blues** (315 Main Street, 601-446-9922), known for smoked ribs and chicken, po-boys, and gumbo. Their Crawfish Beignets were once mentioned in a fictional best selling book set in Natchez and entitled *The Quiet Game* by Greg Iles.

If you love ghosts, then you'll love **Kings Tavern** (619 Jefferson Street, 601-446-8845). While I can't say that I've felt any unusual spirits lurking about my prime rib, others have reported seeing a beautiful young lady. Kings Tavern is said to be the oldest building in the southwest corner of Mississippi and was built by Richardo King, a settler from New York, while Spain occupied the area. The building is constructed with beams from ships no longer fit to sail, dried bricks, and barge boards from the flat boats that came down the Ohio and Mississippi rivers loaded with trade goods. The ambiance downstairs feels very much the way I imagine a sailing ship's galley to be, except there's no rocking. As for the reported ghost sightings, that all started when a grisly discovery was made in the early part of the 20th century. In 1930, repairs had to be made to one of the chimneys and workmen found three bodies encased in the old bricked-up downstairs fireplace. A jeweled dagger was also found, not far from the bodies. The bodies, two males and one female, were not identified but local lore has it that one was Madeline, the young mistress of Richardo King. Identity not withstanding, the haunting hasn't squelched business. You'll find that it will take a bit of time to get your food as the kitchen tries to keep up with the demands of tourists and locals alike. The food is good though and I just loved the tin cups of ice cold water. Kings is open each evening for dinner and during the semi-annual Pilgrimage for lunch. Call ahead for times.

Natchez has a multitude of chain accommodations as well as historic bed-and-breakfast inns. Two that are outstanding are **The Briars** (31 Irving Lane, 800-634-1818, 601-446-9654) and historic **Ravennaside** (601 South Union Street, 601-442-8015), home of Mrs. Roane Fleming Byrnes who almost single-handidly kept the dream of a completed Nashville to Natchez Parkway alive. At one time a free carriage ride through historic downtown Natchez was included in the price of the stay at Ravennaside which ranges from $80 to $135 per night.

If hot air balloons are your thing, then visit during the **Great Mississippi River Balloon Race** (www.natchezballoonrace.com) held each year in late October, which is also an excellent time to ride the Natchez Trace Parkway.

Side Trip: Mammy's Cupboard

If road side oddities rev your throttle, then you'll have to visit **Mammy's Cupboard** (555 Highway 61 North, 601-445-8957, Tuesday through Saturday 11 to 2 p.m.) for at least a photograph. Built in the 1940s as a restaurant and tourist attraction beside a Shell gas station, the building is the brick skirt of a 28-foot tall black woman holding a platter. Alas, Mammy's has succumbed to the ravages of time and political correctness. During a recent renovation she underwent Michael Jackson-type surgery and became, well, almost white! But if she's open, stop in and sample one of her delicious homemade desserts! ■

Trip 20   Natchez to Windsor Ruins

Distance   *126 miles*

Terrain   *Twisty, two-lane road, short section of hard gravel driveway, construction on some parts, well-maintained asphalt on others. Traffic light to moderately light.*

Highlights   *Pastoral views on the Trace, the oldest mansion in Mississippi, the Ruins of Windsor, a huge hand pointing toward the heavens, and the oldest store in southwestern Mississippi*

We start today's journey just north of **Natchez** near the entrance to the **Natchez Trace Parkway** at the intersection of US 84 and US 61. Head north on US 61 for 3.8 miles and take the Natchez Trace Parkway heading north. I've included this 12 mile stretch because the Natchez Trace is a favorite road of mine to ride. The reason isn't the throttle-twisting, knee-dragging curves or

The remoteness of the Ruins of Windsor lends an air of melancholy to the stately columns. But it was a careless smoker instead of the Union Army that caused the destruction.

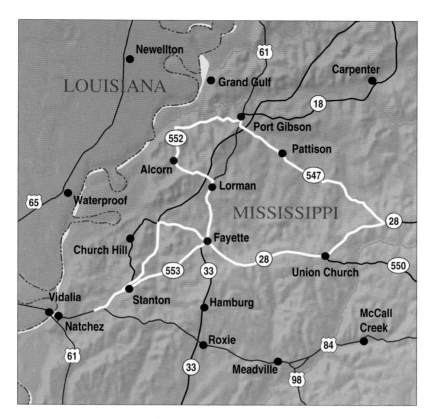

the roller coaster elevation changes common to other parkways in the South. I love the Trace for its history and link with our past. In this book are several other chapters exploring the Trace. But, as you enter this beautiful Parkway here at Natchez, I want you to breathe a "thank you" to Mrs. Roane Fleming Byrnes, who died in 1970, but not before serving for 33 years as the successive president of the Natchez Trace Association. Mrs. Byrnes, more so than any other person, is responsible for keeping the dream of a completed Nashville to Natchez Trace alive. She did not live to see her dream become reality, but we should be grateful for her vision as we ride this beautiful highway.

At Mile 15.7, turn right onto SR 553 and leave the Trace behind. In a few miles you'll come to a faded sign on your left and a gravel drive to **Springfield Plantation** (1833 River Road, 601-786-3802). In 1791, **Andrew Jackson,** before he became our President, married Rachel Donelson Robards in the parlor of the Springfield Plantation. When it was discovered two years later that Rachel was not properly divorced from her first husband, Lewis Robards, the scandal rocked the country.

THE ROUTE FROM NATCHEZ

0	Start on US 61 at US 84
3.8	Enter Natchez Trace Parkway
15.7	Turn right on SR 553 toward Fayette
23.7	Turn left on Main Street
24.0	Turn right on Poindexter Street which becomes Old Hwy 28
25.9	Turn left on SR 28
50.9	Turn left on SR 547 to Port Gibson
76.0	Turn right on US 61 (Church Street)
76.8	Turn left on Carroll Street
77.0	Keep left on Rodney Road
87.0	Turn left to Ruins of Windsor. Turn left on Rodney Road as you depart
89.1	Bear left on SR 552 toward Alcorn
92.1	Stay left on Hwy 552 around Alcorn University
99.0	Turn right to get on US 61/SR 552 and travel south to Lorman
125.	End at US 61 at US 84

Built between 1786 and 1791 Springfield Plantation is supposedly the first mansion built in Mississippi. At the time, this area was known as "West Florida" and was under Spanish Rule. After the rebellion of 1810, the region was annexed into the U.S. Springfield Plantation has been preserved as it was when Jackson and Donelson were married with a few exceptions. The long-time caretaker, Arthur E. LaSalle, also exhibits a lot of his personal memorabilia and is a good and interesting tour guide. While Arthur talks fast, mumbles a lot, is hard to hear, and quite cantankerous, there's just something about getting history from the source. Remember the drive is gravel and can be tricky for large bikes or new riders. Admission to the Plantation is $10 per person.

Continue south on Poindexter Street (old Hwy 28) south for approximately one and a half miles and merge with SR 28. At Mile 51.4, turn left on SR 547 toward the town of **Port Gibson**. In about 25 miles, you'll enter town and spot the **First Presbyterian Church of Port Gibson**. The steeple on this Romanesque Revival style building features a hand with a finger pointing the way toward heaven. The first hand was carved from wood by Daniel Foley which time eventually destroyed, and the new hand, cast from over 2000 pounds of silver coins, was erected in 1901. It was refurbished and replated in 1990.

Leaving the church, return one block to Carroll Street, turn right, and in a couple of blocks, Carroll turns into Rodney Road. Ten miles later you'll come to the entrance of **Windsor Ruins** on your left. Down the short two-rut driveway is the commanding presence of the ruins of Windsor Mansion. All that remains of this stately southern mansion are twenty three burned brick columns standing 45 feet tall, stark contrast to the green grass and blue sky. The story of Windsor Mansion is one of love and loss. **Smith Coffee Daniel II** and his wife Catherine began construction of Windsor in 1859 and it wasn't completed until 1861. Just weeks after its completion, Smith Daniel died at the age of 34. For 29 years the house was the center of culture in the area and was the epitome of the romantic South. Petticoats and silk ascots marked the day and it's not hard to envision the festive gatherings here, just like the ballroom scene in *Gone With The Wind*. Even Mark Twain wrote about Windsor Mansion in his book, *Life on the Mississippi*. In February 1890, a careless house guest dropped a cigarette in some material left by workers who were renovating the third floor and the subsequent fire destroyed everything except the columns. The only rendering of the house as it once stood was done by a Union soldier during the Civil War when it was used as a Union Hospital. During the late afternoon

Before he became president, Andrew Jackson married his wife here at Springfield Plantation in 1791. At the time, neither one knew that she was still married to her first husband.

Buildings like this used to be the center of the universe for folks living in the rural South. The general store was the place where you bought the things that you needed but couldn't grow or build yourself, like nails, candy, coffee, sugar, and flour. Today you won't find hardware, but you will enjoy the best fried chicken within 100 miles.

when the air becomes still and the birds quiet down, you can sit in the shadows of the huge columns and allow your imagination to carry you back to the days when cotton was king, the horse and buggy was transportation, and hoop skirts were high fashion.

Leave Windsor and turn left on Rodney Road. At Mile 89.5, bear left on SR 552 toward **Alcorn** and at Mile 92.5 take the Alcorn bypass left. In seven miles, bear right to merge with US 61 and SR 552 and at Mile 100.5, turn right to visit the **Old Country Store** (18801 Hwy 61, South Lorman, 601-831-2568). The doors to this old establishment first opened in 1895 as a hardware and grocery store that provided the surrounding citizenry with the everyday essentials of life. From coffee to caskets, the Old Country Store served its customers from the cradle to the grave. Today they're serving mashed potatoes and gravy and the finest fried chicken in southwestern Mississippi during the lunch hour.

Side Trip: The Ruins of Rodney

If Arthur Davis, the owner of the Old Country Store is in a good mood you might get him to pencil you a map to the nearby deserted town of **Rodney**. I've been there but the roads were not in

Arthur E. LaSalle is the caretaker for Springfield Plantation and he's as interesting as the house itself.

the best of shape back then so I'd recommend asking a local how to get there and the current road conditions. I wouldn't call Rodney a ghost town per se, because that has a Wild West connotation. Rather Rodney simply dried up in the mid 1800s after two fires, an outbreak of yellow fever, and the shifting channel of the Mississippi River took away its main means of commerce. In 1930 the Governor of Mississippi officially declared the town of Rodney "abolished." If you go, look for the cannon ball lodged in the Presbyterian Church façade.   ■

When you're ready, continue south on US 61 toward Natchez where this journey ends at Mile 126.

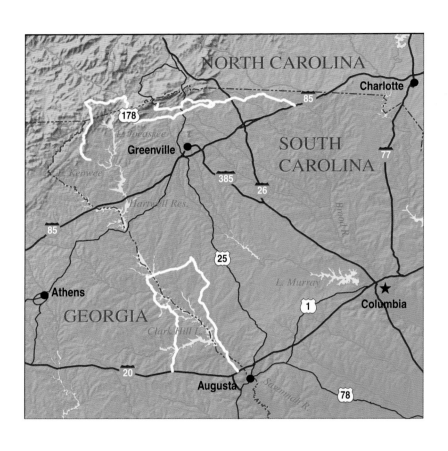

The Southern Carolina

Birthplace of Rebellion

If Ceasars Head was named after the famous Roman Dictator, it took someone with more imagination than I have to see the resemblance.

In the 1600s, **John Locke,** a noted philosopher and metaphysician was asked to draw up a plan to establish a government in the area between Virginia and Florida, an area that would become The Carolinas. In the 120 articles Locke wrote, one of those read, "Carolina shall be divided into counties. Each county shall consist of eight signiories, eight baronies, and four precincts. Each precinct shall consist of six colonies. Each signiory, barony, or colony shall consist of twelve thousand acres. The signiories shall be annexed unalienably to the proprietors; the baronies, to the nobility; and the precincts, being three-fifths of the whole, shall remain to the people." It's noteworthy that Locke was proposing to set aside three-fifths of the land to us common folk.

When I was growing up, every school in the South taught that the first shots of the Civil War were fired at Fort Sumter near Charleston, South Carolina. However, the history books of South Carolina also taught that the real birthplace of the War Between the States is Abbeville. **Abbeville** claims to be the cradle and deathbed of the Confederacy. The deathbed claim is a bit of a stretch (for me). While Jefferson Davis did hold one of his last official "council of war" meetings here, a more appropriate location for the deathbed of the Confederacy would be Atlanta, or Appomattox Courthouse. However, there's no doubt that Abbeville can lay claim to being the place where the idea of southern independence was first acted upon in formal resolution. This strong spirit of what it means to be southern remains undiluted there despite the passage of more than fourteen decades.

However there's more to this adventure than the Civil War. In the upstate of South Carolina we'll visit the **Cowpens Revolutionary Battlefield** site. Located near the town of Gaffney, and a short drive from Interstate 85, the Cowpens stands as a monument to a pivotal and inspirational battle between the well disciplined and outfitted British regulars and the rag-tag Colonial militia fighting to defend its homeland and secure independence for the newly established United States of America. As far as battlefield sites go, there isn't a whole lot to see, except in the museum and visitors center, but there is a restored period home from the era that helps you understand the hardships that faced our forbearers during the early part of our nation's history.

Most of this adventure in Southern Carolina is in what is termed the "Upstate." Using SR 11 (Cherokee Foothills Scenic Drive) as a base, this chapter takes you to a mountain that defeated an ambitious plan to build a railroad from the South Carolina coast to Cincinnati, Ohio. But not all was lost as the uncompleted tunnel turned out to be the ideal location to store cheese!

There is also the ride to **Caesars Head.** No, not the Roman dictator you learned about in World History, but rather the rocky outcropping that lends its name to **Caesars Head State Park** in Cleveland, South Carolina. More on Caesar and how it came to be named later. If you're a covered bridge romantic, you'll love this ride as I'll take you to **Campbell's Bridge,** the last surviving covered bridge in South Carolina. Just so you know, there is another "covered" bridge nearby called **Klickity Klack** which was built in 2000. However Klickity Klack is on private property and wasn't ever used as a transportation artery so it qualifies more as a modern tourist attraction than a historical reference. But, it was still neat to visit!

And speaking of bridges, you'll find out something on this visit that you probably didn't know, and that is the origin of the poinsettia plant. Yes, that perennial Christmas flower has its roots in a bridge out in the middle of nowhere, near the town of **Gowensville,** South Carolina. This trip will take you to the 186 year old stone bridge named for **Joel L. Poinsett,** who is responsible for introducing Americans to the Mexican flower that bears his name.

For those who ride to eat and eat to ride, I've included a few delectable detours in this chapter. My absolute hands-down-favorite is **Strawberry Hill.** Besides being the cleanest eating establishment within 200 miles, Strawberry Hill has the best fried bologna biscuit you will ever sample! Now, if you've read the chapter Sweet Home in this book where I visited Scottsboro, Alabama, and ate fried bologna on the breakfast bar at the Sizzlin Steakhouse, let me explain the difference in the two recipes. Strawberry Hill cuts its bologna thick, probably

Read all about the history of the Cowpens battle site here at the Cowpens National Battlefield Museum in upper South Carolina.

about 1/8 of an inch thick and then lightly fries it on a grill. The Alabama method uses real thin bologna, probably 1/32 of an inch and fries it in a pan, causing it to curl up in the middle. Both are delicious, if you like bologna. (You Northern friends are now probably poking each other in the ribs and making some crude comments about primitive redneck eating habits, but down here we don't care for your fritters, seafood lasagna, or that wonderful breakfast food you call scrapple, which I remind you is made from hog offal—the head, eyes, heart, liver, bladder, and other delectable scraps. Yum Yum!)

Speaking of Yum, in **Cashiers** you'll find **The Grill** (Hwy 64 West), a wonderful traditional southern steakhouse, and at the falls of Toxaway Lake is **October's End Restaurant** (115 Hwy 64 West). The best hot dog on this adventure can be found in Abbeville at **The Rough House** (116 Court Square) but don't expect a huge dog with a loaded bun because you won't find that. Instead, it's a simple boiled frank on a steamed bun. If you're lucky, there'll be some homemade chili to top it off, otherwise just add mustard and ketchup and onions, and top it off yourself with a pack of chips.

For barbeque fanatics, this chapter takes you into **Augusta,** Georgia, which is home to **Sconyers BBQ** (2250 Sconyers Way). Established in 1956 by Claude and Adeline Sconyers, their youngest son, Larry runs the place now

Even if you're not hungry, stop in for a fresh biscuit and homemade strawberry jelly at Strawberry Hill U.S.A. You will be glad you did!

The Bantam Chef is one of those spots where the atmosphere seems to make the food taste even better than it is!

and once served President **Jimmy Carter** and members of Congress at the White House! There's not many barbeque joints with that distinction attached to their resume!

If you never outgrew the 50s, then a visit to the **Bantam Chef** (418 South Alabama Street) in Chesnee, South Carolina, will be your favorite spot on this ride. Besides the hamburgers and fast food, there's a three meat and vegetable lunch that sticks to your ribs like only good ole southern food can!

Admittedly I've only scratched the surface of this great state, but I hope you'll find enough reasons to call in sick, take some vacation time or plan a long weekend, and explore all that The Southern Carolina, or South Carolina as the locals call it, has to offer. Now, let's get started on our adventure.

Trip 21   Abbeville: Cradle of the Confederacy

Distance *134 miles*
Highlights *Birthplace and deathbed of the Confederacy, barbeque fit for a U.S. President, a true southern Opera House, Golf Hall of Fame, and an authentic southern mansion*

We'll begin this journey in **Martinez,** Georgia, a suburb of Augusta. This is one of those rides that you do because you want to say you've been there. There are no twisting mountain roads on this route, or no really great restaurants to speak of, but what it does have is the place where the notion of a free and independent southern nation was born. Regardless of how you view the War of Northern Aggression (and you can see where I come from), this struggle had a monumental impact on the lives of all Americans. Even today the Civil War overshadows small towns everywhere throughout the South as many, in the years following the war, erected granite monuments in their courthouse squares to honor their Confederate dead.

I am intimately familiar with **Augusta,** having spent a number of years employed on its Police Department. It is a city rich in history. Even though The Confederate Powder Works, located on the Augusta Canal, was the largest supplier of gunpowder to the southern cause, Augustans like to say the reason

I discovered Secession Hill quite by accident on a trip to Abbeville, South Carolina. It was on this spot that the first organized meeting was held for the purpose of southern independence.

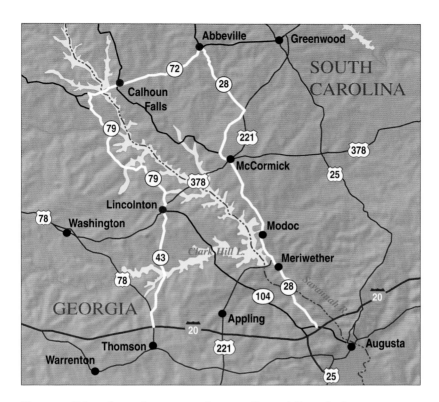

Sherman did not burn the town was because General Grant had a secret sweet-heart here! A more likely reason is that once he finished with Atlanta and made the subsequent march to Savannah, he knew the war was essentially over. There was no need or desire to travel overland to Augusta just to visit more destruction.

Golf fans will tell you Augusta is the home to the world's premier golf championship, **The Masters.** The tournament is played each spring at the very private, well hidden **Augusta National Golf Club** on Washington Road. While you can't tour the National, you can visit the **Georgia Golf Hall of Fame** (11th at Reynolds Street, PO Box 1648, Augusta, 706-724-4443) if you're interested.

Augusta is also home to my favorite barbeque restaurant, **Sconyers BBQ** (2250 Sconyers Way, 706-790-5411). Sconyers once served its famous pork at the White House! If you love barbeque, you have to try this one. It's open Thursday through Saturday from 10 to 10 p.m. and located right off Bobby Jones Expressway. For more Augusta history, I recommend visiting the **Augusta Visitor Information Center** (Inside the Augusta Museum of History, 560B Reynolds Street, 706-724-4067).

THE ROUTE FROM MARTINEZ

0   Riverwatch Parkway SR 104 at Furys Ferry Road (SR 28)
13.8   Right on US 221/28
32.6   Straight on SR 28/221 toward Abbeville
53.6   Right on SR 72/28 into downtown Abbeville
55.8   Left on Secession Avenue
56.0   Marker at Magazine Street and Secession Avenue
56.0   Left on Magazine Street
56.2   Right on SR 20 South Main Street
56.5   Arrive downtown square Abbeville
56.8   Right to stay on SR 20, left into parking lot of Burt Starke Mansion
57.7   Return SR 20 through downtown to turn right on SR 72
59.5   Straight on SR 72 toward Calhoun Falls
85.4   Left on SR 72 toward Lincolnton GA
112.0   Right on US 378 toward Washington
112.3   Left on SR 43
131.6   Left on US 78
134.0   End at I-20 Thomson GA

After exploring Augusta to your heart's content, take **Riverwatch Parkway** to Furys Ferry Road (SR 28) and turn right. Ride 13.8 miles to the town of **Clarks Hill** where US 221 joins SR 28 and then continue on US 221 as it runs along the eastern edge of **Thurmond Lake.** Originally named Clark Hill Lake, this is the largest man-made lake east of the Mississippi. Unfortunately, much of it remains hidden from view as you ride this road.

Remain on US 221 through the town of **McCormick** and at Mile 53.6, bear right to travel into Abbeville. At Mile 55.8, turn left on Secession Avenue and travel a quarter mile up the hill to Magazine Street. At this intersection stands a pair of rather plain pillars with bronze plaques commemorating the Birthplace of the Confederacy, when on November 20, 1860, the first organized secession meeting was held on this hillside. There were six speeches that day and one of those was by a James N. Cochran. I don't know if he was related to me, but you knew I had to mention it! Incidentally there was also a Cochran at The Alamo so I guess we like to stick our noses in history, huh?

Travel west down Magazine Street to South Main Street (SR 20) and turn right at Mile 56.2 to arrive downtown and park on the Court Square. If you could magically silence vehicle traffic (motorcycles included), while visiting the tree-lined Court Square in **Abbeville,** you could easily believe you'd transported back in time to the beginning of the 19th century. The towering monument in the middle looks out over hundreds of buildings in both directions that have been restored or maintained to their original 1850 to 1940 appearance.

If you're up for a spot of billiards and perhaps the best hot dog in a hundred miles, then saunter over to **The Rough House** (116 Court Square, 864-366-1932). A favorite stop for poker runs in this area, the Rough House has been serving residents since 1932 and has the decor and the memorabilia to prove it! Along one wall are seats from the original Opera House before it was renovated. Try the hot dog with chili!

Barbeque Battles

If you're ever in an argumentative mood and looking to pick a good fight, the easiest way to do it is to state definitively that "There's only one way to make barbeque and this is it!" Then go on to describe your method. Someone in the crowd will invariably call you an idiot and the fight's on.

Barbeque can either be a noun or a verb. As a staple of southern politics, the barbeque has no equal. From the White House to the dog house, politicians have used the barbeque to bring supporters together for a pep talk and to renew old friendships and cement new alliances.

In the lard belt of the South the pig is the prince of the spit and while technically you can barbeque any animal (as in verb usage), when using the word as a noun you are referring exclusively to short snout southern swine. In addition to barbeque we have pig pickings, pig pullings, and pig roasts which are all essentially the same thing—a whole hog slow-roasted over hot coals where the meat cooks from the inside out.

Since this is a book about motorcycle travels and not a dissertation on culinary conflicts, I'll leave you with this. There is only one location I believe has the best barbeque in the known universe and it is the same place that in 1979 served its secrets to the President of the United States and guests on the lawn of the White House. The President was **Jimmy Carter** (a fellow Georgian), and the establishment was Sconyers BBQ from Augusta, Georgia. **Sconyers BBQ** (2250 Sconyers Way, 706-790-5411) has been named by *People Magazine* as one of the top ten barbeque restaurants in these United States. For me, it's number 1.   ∎

While you're at it, walk a few doors down and if it's open, tour the **Opera House** (864-366-2157). Opened in 1903, it became an overnight stop for traveling "road companies" that toured between Atlanta and New York. Like many other downtown live theaters, The Opera House fell into disuse once talking movies became popular.

Next to the Opera House is **The Belmont Inn** (104 East Pickens Street, www.belmontinn.net, 877-459-8118). Over 100 years old, the Belmont was originally called the Eureka and served the performing companies at the Opera House as well as salesmen and visitors to Abbeville. If you're still hungry or missed the hot dogs at the Rough House, the **Tinkers Alley Tavern** inside the Belmont serves lunch Monday through Saturday 11:30 to 2 p.m. and dinner Tuesday through Saturday 5 to 9 p.m. The bar is open from 4:30 to Midnight, Monday through Saturday.

The last surviving owner of the Burt-Stark House warned the trustees that she would return to the house on Judgment Day and it had better be in the shape she left it!

Even though the big box retailers draw shoppers away from town squares, the American South still clings to its downtowns and finds ways to entice families back to the heart of its towns.

Before you leave town, you should visit the **Burt-Stark Mansion,** North Main and Greenville Streets, built in 1841 (www.burt-stark.com, 864-366-0166). After Richmond fell to the Union Army, the President of the doomed Confederacy, **Jefferson Davis,** fled to Abbeville and on May 2, 1965 held his final council of war there. He was advised by his remaining Generals that the South had exhausted all its resources and to prolong the fight would only bring more misery and suffering. Davis sadly agreed. He was captured eight days later in **Irwinville** in Southwest Georgia. At the age of 102, the last surviving member of the Stark family, Mary Stark-Davis, admonished the trustees that she planned to return to the house on Judgment Day and everything had better be as she left it! So I wouldn't rearrange any of the furniture while you're on your tour there.

When you're finished touring Abbeville, return south on SR 20 to SR 72 (Greenwood Street) and turn right toward **Calhoun Falls.** After crossing **Richard B. Russell Lake** on the far side of Calhoun twenty miles later, turn left onto SR 79 and head toward **Lincolnton.** Turn right on SR 43, US 378 for a short quarter mile when SR 43 splits off left and continues south. At Mile 126.2, turn left on US 78 toward **Thomson** and the journey's end at Mile 128.7 at I-20. If you're not finished exploring Augusta, head east for the short 25 mile trip back to the **Garden City.**

Trip 22 Hail Caesar: Dog or Roman Politician?

Distance *65.8 miles*

Terrain *Smooth asphalt and flat roads, to medium grade asphalt near Poinsett Bridge. Good, twisty, mountain roads on route to Caesars Head. Traffic is light in most places.*

Highlights *Long meandering roads, the last surviving covered bridge in South Carolina, a bridge that was designed by the man who discovered and brought the poinsettia plant to the USA, the Revolutionary Battlefield site at Cowpens, a pair of 50s diners, and tight twisties up to the top of Caesars Head*

Joel L. Poinsett designed this bridge and by the way, he's also responsible for bringing the Poinsettia plant to America. You would never know it but years ago this bridge was on a well traveled route from Greenville, South Carolina, to Asheville, North Carolina.

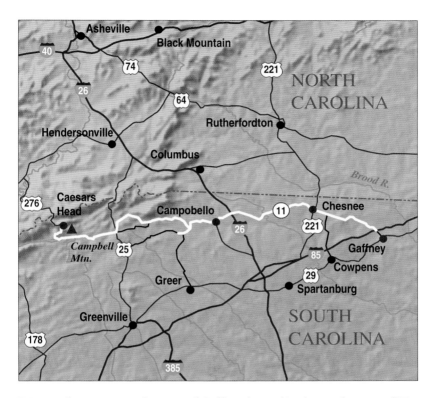

We start this journey in the town of **Gaffney,** located in the area known as "Up-state South Carolina." That's how the locals divide their state and offer quick geographical references. For instance, if you were going to tell a South Carolinian that you were going to take the trip described in this chapter, you would say, "Ah am going to ride the Cherokee Upstate." Say that to someone from New York and they would think you meant to ride your Indian motorcycle to the Catskills!

Gaffney is well known for its peachoid water tank that's located at the intersection of I-85 and SC 11. The whole tank had to be designed from scratch and was the first of its kind in the nation (Alabama now has one). Just the green leaf on the side of the "peach" is over 60 feet long, 16 feet wide, and weighs 7 tons! Even though Georgia officially is known as the "Peach State," it ranks behind South Carolina in the production of that fruit, and Gaffney celebrates that fact with a **Peach Festival** every year. Check www.scpeachfestival.org for more information.

Reset your odometer as you cross I-85 and head west along SR 11, also known as the **Cherokee Foothills Scenic Highway.** In just nine and a half miles you'll come to the gate road for **Cowpens National Battlefield Site** on the left.

THE ROUTE FROM GAFFNEY

0   Start on SR 11 on overpass of I-85

9.5   Turn right into Cowpens National Battlefield Site Park Gate Road

12.0   Turn left on SR 11 leaving Cowpens NBS

14.9   Turn left on Alabama Street in Chesnee

34.0   Turn left on Depot Street

39.3   Turn left on SR 414

41.6   Turn left on SR 114

42.6   Turn left on Pleasant Hill Road and return to SR 414

45.6   Turn left on Smith Road

47.0   Merge left on SR 11

53.7   Turn right on Hwy 912 (Shopping Center Drive)

55.2   Turn right on Calahan Mountain Road

58.5   Turn left on Old Hwy 25

61.7   Turn left on US 25

62.2   Turn right on SR 11

67.3   Turn right on US 276

54.0   Turn right to stay on 11. Turn right on 276 toward town of Caesars Head

65.8   Arrive in town of Caesars Head. Retrace route back on 276 to 11. Turn right on SR 11 to end at West Union

The Revolutionary War battle at The Cowpens in 1781 isn't remembered for its casualties or geographical importance to the fledgling government of the United States. Instead, the victory at Cowpens so inspired the morale of the rebellious colonists that it became one of the most significant battles in the Revolutionary War. Many of the militia from the Carolinas and Georgia carried Pennsylvania's small caliber long rifle developed by the German gunsmiths of that colony. So many of the British officers in the initial exchange of gunfire were killed that it destroyed the proper order of the line and left many regiments leaderless. The ensuing confusion ensured the Patriot victory.

There is a museum and visitors center on site as well as a three mile loop ride around the battlefield. If you decide not to take the loop, you need to adjust the mileage listed. In the park is a restored period dwelling that belonged to Robert and Catherine Scruggs. Sitting just a few feet from the historic Green River Road, the home was built with hand-hewn logs from the area and a hard

Even though I know I have no room on the bike for knick-knacks, I still enjoy browsing in rustic country stores and flea markets like the Country Peddler.

clay filler that served as insulation between the logs. Sitting on the porch, listening to the birds and enjoying the quiet sounds of nature, it's easy to romanticize about what a simple and rewarding life these early settlers must have had. In reality, every day was a struggle to survive. The winters were brutal and unforgiving. There was always wood to chop or animal fat to render into soap. Washing clothes was an all-day chore. You grew what you ate and made what you needed.

When you leave, turn left on SR 11 and in a few miles you'll come to a white building with a red metal roof surrounded by sprawling peach orchids and strawberry fields. This is **Strawberry Hill USA** (3097 Hwy 11 West, 864-461-4000) and if you have the time, stop in and try their breakfast biscuits. I can promise this visit will be one of the highlights of your trip. First off these folks know how to make good iced tea. Their ice is crushed, as proper ice for tea should be, and in the summer, that's as close to heaven as you're likely to find on this side of the grass. If you're a jelly or jam connoisseur your taste buds will slap your tonsils when you slide a piece of their made-from-scratch buttermilk biscuit covered in homemade strawberry jam down your guzzle. I always ask for a couple of extra containers of the jam to take home but if that's not enough for you, larger quantities are available for sale.

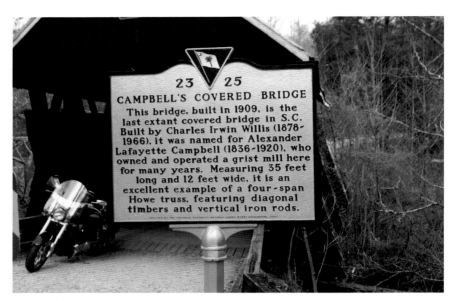

You can't drive over the last existing covered bridge in South Carolina. I eased my bike between the barricades to get this photograph and luckily I didn't get pinched by the historical preservation police.

The decor at Strawberry Hill is purely 50s with chrome accented tables and booths covered in red metal flake vinyl. Best of all it is clean, and I mean military hospital standards clean. As you might guess, my favorite biscuit is fried bologna! Strawberry Hill cuts their bologna so thick it could be called "bologna steak." I'm used to bologna fried thin and greasy, but this method definitely has its merits. In fact, I think I'm in love. There's also butter, bacon, sausage, ham, chicken, and gravy biscuits, or any combo thereof. Oh, and a liver mash biscuit that I'm still trying to convince my taste buds would be a "walk on the wild side." They've threatened to strike.

In addition to the restaurant, there's an ice cream stand in the rear along with a limited item convenience store with gasoline. If that's not enough to pique your interest, the owners have a baby grand player piano that sits in the middle of all of this, continuously tinkling out an assortment of tunes. Sure it's eclectic, but it's also refreshingly southern. Before you leave, head to the back of the store near the ice cream to read the newspaper account of the owner's motorcycle wreck in 2003. His story will inspire and warm your heart.

When you've had your fill, continue west on SR 11 to the town of **Chesnee** and at Mile 14.9, turn left on Alabama Street. On the right is the **Bantam Chef** (418 South Alabama Street, 864-461-8403). If you're still lost in the 50s, this will be another culinary delight. Open from 6 a.m. to 10 p.m. daily the Chef serves the usual fast food and a three meat and vegetable lunch. It's worth a stop to see the restored Studebaker, the restored BMW three wheeler, and the old Harley-Davidsons on display. When you leave, retrace your route north on Alabama Street to SR 11 and turn left.

At Mile 34 just outside the town of **Campobello,** turn left onto Depot Street to head into town. In less than a mile you'll pass right by the **Country Peddler** on your right (305 Depot Street, 864-468-5200), which is open Tuesday through Saturday 10 to 5 p.m. If you love antiques and or er…junk…then this authentic country store and bargain barn will delight you to no end. If you're the kind of person who spends hours at flea markets then you might want to save this stop and return in a car or truck because you're bound to find something inside that you didn't know you had to have until you did. The present owners say the building was once a store, then a church and a restaurant, and now just a collection of things we threw away just a few years ago.

Continue west to South Main Street (US 176) and turn right to the **Dutch Plate Restaurant and Catering** (206 Main Street, 864-468-4584) on your right. It's a local favorite featuring Pennsylvania Dutch home cooking and a gift shop. Continue north for a couple of blocks, pick up SR 11 again, and turn left to head west. At Mile 39.3 in **Gowensville,** turn left onto SR 414 for the

The Klickity Klack Bridge was built just because its owner decided to build a covered bridge. It has no other purpose, but bikers understand that because we take rides to nowhere just because we like to ride.

first stop on our "three centuries of bridges" tour. At Mile 41.6, turn left on SR 114 and in just over a mile turn left on Pleasant Hill Road. In a couple hundred feet you'll come to Campbell Bridge Road on your right. If you go too far and cross Beaver Dam Creek you can access Campbell's Bridge at the next right turn. **Campbell's Covered Bridge** was built in 1909 and those who study covered bridges will instantly note that the bridge is an excellent example of a four-span Howe truss design which features diagonal timbers and vertical rods. The rest of us are just happy that the last surviving covered bridge in South Carolina still stands for us to enjoy and admire. Retrace your route to 114 and after returning the short distance to SR 414, continue north on SR 414 to Mile 45.6 and turn left on Smith Road. In one and a half miles you'll merge with SR 11, turn left, and come to the second covered bridge on today's route, the **Klickity Klack**. Built in 2000, Don Spann and Troy Coffey built the bridge with help from Old Blue, their trusty tractor. One word of advice, if you're the kind of person who has to ride over everything just to say you did it (like me), take the road around the back of the bridge and come in from the rear. The steep right hand 90 degree slow speed downhill turn is a little tricky to pull off. Better yet, park your bike in front, snap the photo, and then turn it around without going over the bridge.

This is what happens when you allow third graders to name highways.

Flea Markets

Flea Markets derived from the French *"marche aux puces,"* named after the outdoor bazzar in Paris, France, of the same name. Flea markets have been around for hundreds of years and the term became popular because of that pesky blood sucking parasite. Before the home exterminator became ubiquitous, the outdoor bazaar is where the rich would dispose of their upholstered furniture once it became flea-infested. Hence, the unflattering term, flea market. While we hardly notice them, visitors from outside the region will undoubtedly think that there are an over abundance of these establishments in the South. Notwithstanding the show "Flea Market Finds" on cable, I don't think we have any more than anywhere else in the country. What we do have in the South is the "world's longest outdoor flea market." Held in mid-August each year, US 127 becomes a huge bargain shopper's paradise. Stretching from Covington, Kentucky, through Jamestown, Tennessee (where it all began), to its end 450 miles later in Gadsden, Alabama, there is something for every taste. For more information, call 800-327-3945. ∎

Continue west on SR 11 for a little over five miles to Mile 53.7 and turn right on Hwy 912. In just over 1.6 miles, turn right on Callahan Mountain Road to the **Poinsett Bridge,** named for its designer Joel L. Poinsett, who served as the U.S. ambassador to Mexico from 1825 to 1829 and introduced an unknown Mexican flower, the **Poinsettia Pulcherrina** to our country. Park on the left side of the road in the hard packed dirt.

Spanning an insignificant stream of water on a little traveled rural road, the Poinsett Bridge is all but forgotten by history. Once an important part of the State Road from Greenville, South Carolina, to Asheville, North Carolina, today the site is neglected and in need of an infusion of cash to make it more tourist friendly. It is a fascinating landmark for me though. I love to stand in its quiet midst and listen to the sounds of Calahan Branch as it flows underneath the intricately placed rock archway. I marvel at the workmanship of the builders and the simplicity and strength of Poinsett's design. For almost 200 years this bridge has witnessed the passing of the seasons. Save a geological disaster, I'd wager it will survive for another 200 years.

If you continue down Calahan Mountain Road a little over two miles, you'll come to Old Hwy 25 at Mile 58.5. Turn left and you'll shortly come to US 25. Turn left again and in .5 miles you'll return to SR 11. Turn right on SR 11.

Located on the historic Green River Road this 1700s dwelling is a monument to simplicity and the solitude of rural life in upstate South Carolina.

At Mile 67.3, where SR 11 joins with US 276, turn right and follow US 276 up **Campbell Mountain** to **Caesars Head State Park.** For the sportbike or sport touring reader this will be the perfect end to a good day's ride. The only thing better than the tight twisties heading up the mountain is knowing you'll enjoy them again on the return trip down. In a few miles, you'll come to a parking area with access to a large flat rock outcropping on your right. The view from this bald mountain rock is spectacular and you are welcome to walk as far as you dare, which isn't much of a dare because the slope is so gentle you could actually make the entire descent without breaking out your climbing gear. (What? You don't carry climbing gear in your saddlebags? Shame on you.) As you enjoy the view, watch out for the nails and such that are in the hollows and depressions where campers have built fires and spent nights out enjoying a view of the heavens above the haze of civilization. Don't worry though, the parking lot is thankfully free from nails. This is an excellent spot for a late day picnic so if you planned ahead, break out the cheese, crackers, and Nehi sodas and sit for a spell.

When you're rested, continue up the mountain to reach **Caesars Head State Park** (8155 Greer Highway, Cleveland, 864-836-6115). At the previous overlook the view was on the eastern side of the mountain. Here you will enjoy an expansive view of the western side. If you're so inclined you can take the easy hike (really easy, trust me) to the various vantage points. If you're

During the day the foothills of upstate South Carolina stretch out in all directions. At night campfires dot this rocky outcropping and the heavens become a blanket of stars.

claustrophobic, I wouldn't recommend traversing the **Devils Kitchen** but there is a bypass around to the other side to get a good look at the rock outcropping that is said to resemble that famous Roman guy for which the park is named.

There is, however, a little controversy over the actual origin of the name, and now's a good time as any for me to weigh in with my two cents worth. I've looked at this rock outcropping every way to Sunday and I can't for the life of me think that it resembles any rendering of Caesar that I've ever seen. One local theory is that the area is named for a favorite coon dog who fell to his death during a nighttime hunt. I don't buy that, because I don't believe any self-respecting coon hunter would name his dog Caesars Head. I do think that there was a coon dog named Caesar, though, and once during a hunt, this dog treed a coon so big that he'd make three of that coon dog's head. Of course, the coon got away, but because of his size, he became legendary as time passed. The tale of the giant coon naturally spread far-and-wide until Upstate hunters began to refer to the area as the spot where that big ole coon, "ten times bigger than Caesar's head," lived. Over time it just got shortened to Caesars Head. Now, I know you readers are shaking your heads in disbelief, but trust me on this, having grown up in the South, truth is sometimes stranger than fiction.

Time to head back down the mountain on SR 276 and return to the intersection of SR 11. Turn right and continue on to the end of the Cherokee Foothills Scenic Highway.

Trip 23 Stumphouse to Toxaway Run

Distance *104 miles*
Terrain *Tight mountain twisties with good asphalt, elevation changes from foothills to mountain gorges. Traffic is moderate for first part of trip, heavy in the middle, and moderate in the final section.*
Highlights *Tunnel to nowhere, mountain scenery, Toxaway Dam*

We'll start the day's journey in **Walhalla,** South Carolina. Before you leave town, ride down Church Street where you'll see the **"Jail on Wheels."** In the early part of the last century it wasn't practical or possible for inmate work crews to reach the outer edges of the county in the morning and return by dark. So many penal officials came up with innovative ways of securing their prisoners at night. Oconee County came up with a 14-foot long, 8-foot wide and 7-foot high rolling cage to house prisoners overnight. Twelve men would sleep on metal bunks in the cage, sweating in the summer and shivering in the winter, although there was a metal barrel in the middle for a fire. Don't ask about bathroom facilities.

Cherokee Foothills Scenic Highway is an excellent alternative to I-85. It runs 115 miles from the Georgia/South Carolina border up to Gaffney.

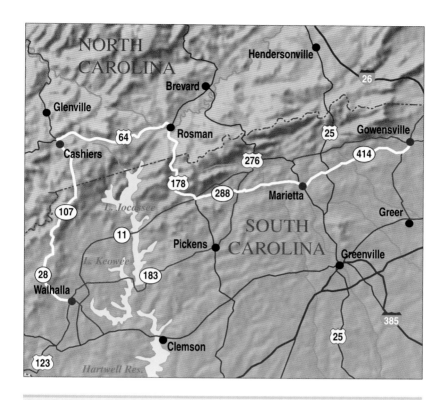

THE ROUTE FROM WALHALLA

0	Start on SR 183 at SR 28 in Walhalla, South Carolina
5.8	Turn right on Stumphouse Mountain Tunnel Road
6.3	Turn right on SR 28
8.5	Bear right on SR 107 toward Cashiers, North Carolina
31.7	Turn right on US 64 in Cashiers
43.8	October's End Restaurant
51.3	Turn right on US 178 (Old Rosman Highway)
68.2	Turn left on SR 288 (Table Rock Road) toward Marietta
83.2	Turn right on US 276
84.7	Turn left on SR 414 (Bates Crossing Road)
88.8	Turn left for a couple hundred feet on US 25/414
88.9	Turn right on SR 414
103.9	End at SR 11 (Cherokee Foothills Scenic Drive)

It was at this tunnel where Stumphouse Mountain defeated the dreamers who tried to build a railroad from South Carolina to Cincinnati.

You'll also want to check out the telephone connector building behind the police station. When phone service was first introduced, you didn't dial the number directly, you called the exchange and told them who you wanted to talk to and they connected you, sometimes eavesdropping in as well. The building is not open to the public yet, but hopefully the funds will be found to restore it as a telephone museum.

From North Catherine Street (SR 183), head north on E. Main (SR 28). As you climb **Stumphouse Mountain,** watch for the entrance to **Stumphouse Mountain Tunnel** on your right at Mile 5.9. Turn right and drive to the gate at the bottom. Park and walk the short gravel stretch to this mountain that proved too tough to tunnel through.

The original plan of the tunnel builders was to construct a railroad between Charleston, South Carolina, and Cincinnati, Ohio. Stumphouse was one of thirteen tunnels needed to carry the railroad across the **Blue Ridge Mountains.** Designed to be over 5,800 feet long, only 4,363 feet of the tunnel was ever completed because after the Civil War, the State of South Carolina couldn't sell the bonds necessary to continue to fund the project. For decades, various visionaries tried to revive the project in some manner probably because 80 percent of the groundwork had been completed. When **Fontana Dam** was built in North Carolina in the 1940s, it flooded much of the **Little Tennessee Valley** and forever closed the chapter on the rail line connecting Charleston to Cincinnati. The tunnel found use for a time as a unique research facility.

If you want to see the pick axe marks left by the Irish workers on the walls and floors of the uncompleted Stumphouse Mountain Tunnel, you'll need to bring a flashlight. The Civil War and a dam in North Carolina put an end to the dream of this railroad.

Because the temperature inside remains a constant 50 degrees with 85 percent humidity, nearby **Clemson University** used Stumphouse to store and age blue cheese, until they were able to duplicate the temperature and conditions at the University's Agricultural Center and the cheese making operation was relocated. The brick room, in the back, remains in place and you can visit it. But, there are no lights in the tunnel so bring a flashlight. If you stand still back in the tunnel and listen to the ground water as it drips from the ceiling, you can almost hear the Irish immigrants with their big pick axes striking at the granite walls hour after hour, day after day. They worked 12 hours a day, six days a week. Plainly visible on the sides of the tunnel are the deep gouges left by these tunnel workers as they used hand drills, sledge hammers, and black powder, but still progressed only 200 feet per month.

Leaving Stumphouse Tunnel, turn right to continue up the mountain and in less than a mile at the crest of the mountain stands the **Mountain Top Trading Post.** Most motorcyclists passing through stop in for boiled peanuts or a cool refreshing drink. The owner's Harley-Davidson will most likely be sitting outside. So no matter what, stop in and say hi.

Continue on SR 28 through the **Sumter National Forest** and at Mile 8.5, bear right on SR 107 and 22 miles later you'll arrive in the town of Cashiers, North Carolina. You'll enjoy this stretch of highway as long as traffic is light. That has a lot to do with the tourist season and early spring, the dead of winter,

If you need directions or just want to stop and chat, the owner of the Mountain Top Trading Post owns the Harley you'll see parked out front, and is happy to spend some time chatting with you.

I like this view of the spillway of Lake Toxaway as seen from the deck of October's End Restaurant.

and late fall are the least congested. Temperatures in the winter can be downright brutal and black ice often forms on the road so that's not the best time for this route.

In **Cashiers** you have an abundance of choices for restaurants and you won't be disappointed in any of these. If unique is your cachet, then try **Cornucopia** (Hwy 107, 828-743-3750) open seven days a week during the season. **The Grill** (828-743-1180) is located in the Ingles Shopping Center on Hwy 64 West and is a traditional southern steakhouse. For barbeque it's got to be the **Carolina Smokehouse** (828-743-3200) also on Hwy 64 West, open Monday through Saturday 11 to 9 p.m. They serve more than just barbeque but that's their specialty! Life in Cashiers used to be typical of most mountain towns, slow and predictable. The area has, in recent years, undergone a transformation as retirees from the cities discovered the charm and beauty of this lush green valley situated 3,500 feet above sea level.

Leaving Cashiers, head east on US 64 toward **Toxaway Lake.** This will be the worst part of this journey, even though it's twisty and would normally be a joy to ride, the traffic is almost always heavy. It's only 12 miles through so take your time, watch out for vacationers entering and leaving driveways, and you'll be fine. At Mile 43.7, turn right into the parking lot of **October's End Restaurant,** (115 Highway 64 West, 828-966-9226). From their veranda you can get

Chain Gangs

Forcing prisoners to work in chain gangs wasn't unique to the South, but its use was widespread in the region during the late 1800s and continued right up to the late 60s. The purpose of the gangs wasn't economical, as the value of the work performed was worth less than the expense of maintaining the gangs. The main reason for the gangs was the deterrent effect. The sight of prisoners working in oppressive conditions was supposed to deter potential miscreants from a life of crime. The movie, *O Brother Where Art Thou* released in 2000 is a somewhat accurate portrayal of the southern penal system during the Depression.   ■

a glimpse of the falls at Lake Toxaway. The crew at October's End is friendly and it's a local favorite; Having gotten its unusual name from the fact that years ago it served the summer vacationing crowd and would close October 31st for the winter. However, the area now has many more permanent residents and consequently the restaurant remains open year-round. Time for a name change I reckon!

Continue west on US 64 and you'll soon cross an imaginary boundary from **Nantahala National Forest** into **Pisgah National Forest,** although the scenery won't change much as you climb **Quebec Mountain.** Nantahala is Native American for "land of the midday sun" and it's appropriate for a forest in this area of deep gorges and steep mountain ranges where some areas only see the sun during its zenith. Keep this in mind if you're traveling the area during the months when the temperatures drop below freezing at night. I've said this before but it bears repeating that the temperatures may be in the mid or upper 40s but there will be shady areas that don't thaw out on those days. Ride with caution.

At Mile 51.2, turn right on US 178 (Old Rosman Hwy) and head south toward the South Carolina line and up and over **Sassafras Mountain.** I always enjoy this leg of the journey. 17 miles later you'll cross SC 11 (Cherokee Foothills Scenic Drive) and turn left on SR 288 (Table Rock Road) heading to the town of **Marietta.** At Mile 83.2, turn right onto US 276 for one and a half miles and at Mile 84.7, turn left on SR 414. At Mile 89.4, turn left on US 25 for a few hundred feet and turn back right on SR 414. Turn left on SR 14, and the ride ends at the junction of SR 11 in the town of **Gowensville.**

"Hey, All Y'all, Listen Up"

Having grown up in rural Georgia, I feel I'm qualified to explain the southern expressions you will probably hear when you visit this region.

Y'all: This is short for "you all" which is plural, always. If you're by yourself in a restaurant and a waitress asks you, "What would y'all like to drink?", this is natural. Southerners are deeply religious people and believe that God is with you always. So no matter if you're the only person at the table, the waitress is including God in the question.

All y'all (pronounced Aw Yawl): Short for everyone in hearing distance. Sometimes it's necessary to clarify that everyone who can hear you is included. For instance, you may be at a party where there are several groups of people talking amongst themselves and to make sure everyone knows you're speaking to them, you would say, "Hey, all y'all, listen up…wrestling is fixing to start on TV."

Fer: Same as "for"

Fixin' to: Beginning, starting, impending, as in, "I'm fixin to leave, are you ready?"

Bode-up also Bowed up: To take offense and show it, or to threaten physically. Confrontation, as in: "he was fixin to bode-up on me before you showed up."

Catywompus: Sideways or askew, as in, "If he woulda bowed up on me I'da knocked him catywompus up side the head." *Not used much anymore.*

Hear tell: You heard it from someone else: As in, "I hear tell y'all found a new restaurant with some might fine victuals."

Victuals, or Vittals: Food, supper, breakfast, any meal.

Pie (pronounced Paah): As in, "Let's have some homemade pie."

No count: Not good for anything. Lazy, sorry, as in, "I hear tell your sister married that no count biker dude from down the way."

Tarnation: Surprise, shock, displeasure as in "What in tarnation did your sister marry that no count biker fer?"

Accidental Discoveries

Friends often comment that I am the luckiest person when it comes to finding unique and out of the way places to ride and while I don't discount that luck has a lot to do with it sometimes, I also know that having a curious nature helps a lot as well. While following the routes given in this book will direct you to the interesting and unique places I have found, I encourage you to develop your own ability to find these sorts of destinations. There's really no secret to it, except this. Always be willing to take the road less traveled, and pay attention to the clues. If I'm riding along and see a road named "Watson Mill Bridge Road" and don't know where it goes, I'm going to detour down and see where it leads, if it's paved. In the early days of our nation, road names evolved from geographic features or businesses and landmarks on them. Hence, Watson Mill Bridge has a bridge that was located at Watson's Mill. The mill is gone, but the covered bridge is still there.

Sometimes this takes me on a path to nowhere. I remember when I was in Natchez and scouting around for new roads I took an unfamiliar highway that looked promising on the map. A couple miles later I started grinning from ear to ear as I realized this road was a sportbiker's dream. A stretch of good pavement twisting and turning, up and down through gnarled oaks and ten foot red clay cliffs on either side. The best part was I hadn't seen another vehicle in the past three miles. I started thinking up adjectives to describe this route when I crested a hill and saw to my dismay the end of the asphalt and a dirt gravel road. I was so disappointed that I continued down the gravel road for a quarter mile or so just in case the pavement picked up on the other side. But, no luck. If I had the money I would finish paving that road myself, it was that good. If you're thinking I wasted time chasing a road to nowhere, then maybe you're better off leaving the exploration to someone else. For me, I wouldn't have it any other way.

It's the Heat and Humidity

I'm sure you've heard the saying, "it's not the heat, it's the humidity." Well, to an extent this is true. Riding in the summer in 98 degree temperatures with 98 percent humidity is brutal because you just can't seem to sweat enough to get cool. The reason is the humidity. When you sweat your body is trying to use evaporative cooling to lower your core temperature. If your sweat doesn't evaporate because the air is holding about all the moisture it can, then you won't cool off efficiently.

This brings me to how to dress to ride in the South in the summer. My first advice is "don't ride in the South in the summer until you become acclimatized to the humidity and the heat." When you've done that, here are a few tips to help you ride more comfortably:

1. If you ride behind a windshield, remove it. The heat building up behind the windscreen will transform your ride into something resembling a day with your head stuck in an oven. If removing the windshield isn't an option, then stop often and use cold water to cool off. I often wear a long sleeve, lightweight, white tee shirt that I soak down with water at gas stops as soon as I start to feel the effects of the heat. The long sleeves keep the exposed skin on my arms from literally cooking in the sun. I also carry a spare short sleeve shirt to change into whenever I get to my destination if I plan on being outside.

2. Drink water. Repeat, drink water. Your body is losing water at a rapid pace, and once you feel thirsty you've gone too long. Watch your urine. If it's dark yellow, you're in the first stages of dehydration. Drink more water. Skip the beer; it just causes you to lose more water.

3. Consider wearing a full face helmet, rather than a beanie hat. Depending on the brand, you might actually be cooler wearing a full face helmet. I know you might think I'm suffering from the effects of a heat stroke but it's true. Here's how I do it. Soak one of those water absorbing wraps in ice water and place it around the base of your helmet. Open all the vents on a high quality full face and shut the visor. The cool air will keep your face, neck, and head cooler than it would if they were exposed to the sun and hot wind. BUT, this only works if you're taller than your windshield or you don't have a windshield and you've paid the money for a GOOD helmet. I'm talking in the $300 to $500 range. My favorite is a flip face helmet but not all are created equal.

Animals, Insects, & Hostile Plants

Kudzu: Contrary to what you have heard, Kudzu will not completely ensnare you if you take a nap near it. While it grows fast, sometimes up to 18 inches in one day, it's not an attack vine out to ensnare unsuspecting travelers. The only plant you should be cautious of is **poison ivy** and **poison oak**. Remember the old adage, "leaflets three, let it be!"

Fire Ants: You will probably encounter seemingly innocuous mounds of dirt in your travels in the South. These are the blackish-reddish fire ants which were accidentally imported from Brazil in cargo arriving in Mobile, Alabama, in the 1930s. If you tangle with these tiny, ill-tempered insects, you will surely come away worse for the wear. They swarm voraciously over anything that disturbs their mound and have been known to kill small mammals with thousands of stings. The best way to avoid them is to simply watch for and stay clear of the mounds. If you feel the ground beneath your foot give way for a couple of inches, immediately step back and see if you've disturbed a mound. If you have, you'll see them swarming around the mound; but don't panic, simply step away and stamp your feet a couple times to dislodge any fire ants that may have attacked your boots. The danger is stepping in a mound and standing there. By the time you feel the first sting, you will be bitten a hundred times before you can take off your clothing to get to them and dislodge them. And trust me, you will take off whatever is necessary to get them off of you. I know, I've done it. Fire ants won't kill a human, unless you have a severe allergic reaction, anaphylaxis, to their venom, which isn't very likely. Signs of anaphylaxis can include dizziness, nausea, sweating, low blood pressure, headache, and shortness of breath. Antihistamine and corticosteroids are used as first aid as well as a 50 percent bleach solution to the affected area, but nobody I know carries bleach in their saddlebags so that might be useless information.

Snakes: There are four major types of poisonous snakes and the South has them all—the Coral, Copperhead, Cottonmouth (Water Moccason), and Rattlesnake. Your chance of encountering any one of these creatures is very slim, and since most bikers wear leather boots, you're already ahead in the protection department. Just watch under and around your feet when you're hiking or exploring off the motorcycle, and you'll be fine. Myth buster: Cottonmouth snakes will not pursue you if you run, and rattlesnakes don't wait on branches of overhanging trees to drop on unsuspecting motorcyclists.

Deer: Out of all of Mother Nature's hazards facing motorcycle riders, deer top the list. Often active in the late afternoon and early evening hours, encounters with deer cause a lot of accidents and unfortunately some fatalities. The fall is perhaps the most dangerous time, as that is the mating season. When the bucks are chasing the females, they're often oblivious to traffic. Loud pipes do not help! Also in our winter the roadside offers green grass that tends to draw deer to graze. Unfortunately, there is little you can do to avoid encounters, except slow down and watch carefully for them during the evening and at night. If you see one deer cross in front of you the odds are there are two or three more in the ditch or woods getting ready to cross too, so SLOW DOWN! If you see deer grazing on the side of the highway, don't blow your horn, hoping to scare them into the woods; it just might scare them into your path. Instead, slow down, give them a wide berth, and expect them to react in an unexpected manner. One tip: after slowing down, flick your high beams if a deer continues to stand motionless, staring at you. They are curious animals and can become "fixated" on a moving object. Once you've broken their gaze, they will usually move off to the security of the woods and you can pass safely.

Insects: If there's one thing we have plenty of, it's bugs. Most are simply annoying and pose no significant threat. As a general rule, bugs are most active the hour before sunset and up to one hour after sunrise, although I try not to be up that early to be annoyed by them. Once while enroute to a Harley Owners Rally in Jekyll Island, I was traveling through the small town of Ludowici, Georgia. While crossing a railroad track, I suddenly felt something large crawling up my leg! With my left hand, I grabbed that area to isolate it from other sensitive parts and tried to pull off the street one handed into a parking lot. I couldn't pull in the clutch without letting go of whatever it was in my pants so I just let the bike choke down, almost dumping it in the process. I don't know how I got the kickstand down but I remember hastily jumping off the bike, still holding my jeans and whatever it was inside them, and with my free hand unbuckling my belt and dropping my pants to get at the invader. As it turns out, it was the largest click beetle I have ever seen, at least three inches long! With the immediate emergency past, I began to assess my surroundings. That's when I realized I was directly across from the Police station with my pants down around my boots and an uh-oh look on my face. I didn't bother inspecting the spot to see if I'd been bitten, or if there was another bug, I just pulled up my jeans, and tried to leave as quietly as my straight pipes would allow.

Flags of the Confederacy

Controversy and Confusion

There is no other symbol in this country that causes as much controversy as the 1863 Confederate Navy Jack Flag, which is known today as the Battle Flag of the Confederacy. Its origin can be traced to William Porcher Miles, a former mayor of Charleston, South Carolina, who, during his membership in the Confederate Provisional Congress, chaired the "Committee on the Flag and Seal" which adopted the first national flag called the Stars and Bars. This flag, designed with a blue canton and white stars, on a field consisting of one white horizontal bar between two red horizontal bars was hard to distinguish from the flag of the United States. During the first major battle of the war, Confederate Generals complained they could not tell friend from foe on the battlefield. Eventually, the Confederacy adopted two flags, a parade or peace time flag and a "battle flag," which is today the most universally recognized symbol of the American South. Here's a trivia note. Public display of this or any flag of the Confederacy was illegal during Reconstruction while Federal troops occupied a state. It is unfortunate that a piece of cloth from our past, which should be viewed as a symbol of respect for the gallant struggle of our ancestors, has been usurped by individuals and groups for purposes never intended by its creators. Former Georgia Governor Roy Barnes lost re-election when he pushed through an unpopular flag redesign which removed all references to the Confederate flag from the Georgia flag. Today, Mississippi is the only state flag which retains the Confederate Navy Jack as a part of its flag.

However, there is another flag which first inspired the rebellious nature of southerners and it was a flag with a lone star on a field of blue, and it wasn't in Texas. It was the Independent Republic of West Florida. Curiously, West Florida wasn't where you'd expect it to be, as it encompassed almost half of Mississippi, parts of Lower Alabama, and northern Louisiana stretching all the way to the Gulf of Mexico. West Florida's history began in 1800 when Spain returned the Louisiana colony to the French without specific boundaries. The U.S. claimed the region in the 1803 Louisiana Purchase but Spain disputed that claim. In the meantime U.S. settlers moving into the region resisted Spanish rule resulting in a rebellion in 1810. The rebels took the garrison at Baton Rogue and unfurled a flag that consisted of a single white star on a field of blue, which would become known as the Bonnie Blue Flag. While the Republic of

West Florida only lasted less than 90 days, its flag later inspired the Lone Star flag of Texas and also the flag of California. When Mississippi ceded from the Union during the War Between the States, it raised the Bonnie Blue Flag over the capitol city of Jackson. Harry McCarthy was present and wrote the song, *Bonnie Blue Flag*. The song became a popular marching song and the flag became the unofficial flag of the Confederacy. Movie buffs will recall that in *Gone With the Wind*, Rhett Butler calls his newborn daughter Bonnie Blue Butler, because it was said that her eyes were as blue as the Bonnie Blue Flag.

Hurray! Hurrah!
For Southern Rights, Hurrah!
Hurrah for the Bonnie Blue Flag
That bears a Single Star!

Index

About the Author

Raised in rural Keysville, Georgia, Scott Cochran first learned to ride a motorcycle without his parents' knowledge or permission.

He's always been fascinated by the history of the American South, so besides looking for exciting and fun motorcycle roads to ride, he also tries to discover something unique about the area he's in.

While admitting he wasn't a very good student in high school, he did, however, have an English Literature teacher who insisted he memorize poems or excerpts from great literary figures in history. The one he remembers most is Robert Frost's *The Road Not Taken.* That stuck with him and over the years, taking the *road less traveled* has become his mantra.

Scott is married to Sylvia Cochran and they have four children: Scott Cochran Jr., Ron Moore, Lesley Moore, Jason Cochran, and one grandson, Weston Moore. Scott and Sylvia publish *USRiderNews* and also produce USRiderTV, which currently airs on Dish Network.